TINIE TEMPAH

MY STORY SO FAR

1 3 5 7 9 10 8 6 4 2

First published in 2011 by Ebury Press, an imprint of Ebury Publishing
A Random House Group company

The Random House Group Limited Reg. No. 954009

Addresses for companies within the Random House Group can be found at
www.randomhouse.co.uk

A CIP catalogue record for this book is available from the British Library

The Random House Group Limited supports The Forest Stewardship Council (FSC®), the leading
international forest certification organisation. Our books carrying the FSC label are printed on FSC®
certified paper. FSC is the only forest certification scheme endorsed by the leading environmental
organisations, including Greenpeace. Our paper procurement policy can be found at www.
randomhouse.co.uk/environment

Printed and bound in Great Britain by Butler Tanner & Dennis Ltd, Frome, Somerset

ISBN 9780091945237

To buy books by your favourite authors and register for offers visit www.randomhouse.co.uk

CONTENTS

Good morning, afternoon and evening!
Welcome to my weird and wonderful world.
So glad you could join me on the rollercoaster ride that has been the past 18 months. I've achieved things that I thought wouldn't be possible and have lived out some of my wildest dreams: Number 1 singles and albums, MOBOs, BRITs and Ivor Novellos and collaborating and touring with some of the biggest artists in the world! None of which (of course) would have been possible without all of your support.

I really hope you enjoy reading this book as much as I have enjoyed putting it together; to follow are some of the most personal pictures and memories of the last 22 years of my life (even the embarrassing ones!)

Thanks so much for making my dreams come true and remember to always follow your dreams no matter how crazy they seem!

One love
your boy

THIS BOOK IS DEDICATED TO ALL THE SCHOOLS I WENT TO: ST FRANCIS', ST PATRICK'S, ST PAUL'S, AND ST FRANCIS XAVIER SIXTH FORM. YOU GUYS TAUGHT ME HOW TO READ BOOKS AND NOW I'VE WRITTEN ONE!

Chapter One:

LDN BOY

"SITTING IN MY DAD'S OLD BARBER SHOP, I USED TO PULL FACES WHEN HE PASSED THE MOP."

Growing Up

Okay, let's start at the very, very, very beginning. Well, I was born Patrick Chukwuemeka Okogwu Jr. in Guy's Hospital, central London, on Monday, 7th November 1988 to my parents, Rosemary and Patrick Sr. My middle name means 'God is great' in the Nigerian Igbo language. I'm very proud of that and even though it's a tough one to say when you're little, I'm very thankful to my parents for giving me that name.

I'm incredibly close to my mum and dad and even to this day I still find myself calling them Mummy and Daddy! During my birth, I popped out quite easily apparently. My little sister Marian was the one who caused my mum some trouble. I've got another younger sister called Kelly and a younger brother, Kelvin, so I was the first of quite a big family.

Back then we lived on the Aylesbury Estate in Peckham, south-east London. My very, very first memory – this is embarrassing – was when I was about three years old. My mum let my hair grow out really, really long; she just couldn't bear to cut my baby hair. Around that time, my dad's sister came over to stay with us for a while. One day when my mum was out, my aunt took it upon herself to cut off all of my hair! I remember my mum came home and she screamed the whole place down. Mum calmed down after a while and decided I probably needed a hair cut anyway, and we all laugh about it now.

My hair isn't my only embarrassing memory from when I was a kid though. My mum used to like to dress all us kids up the same. My sister Kelly is just a year younger than me and Mum would always try to make us wear matching tops or jumpers.

My extended family is absolutely massive. My mum has nine brothers and sisters, some of them married into different races and cultures and every one of them has kids, so in total I have a great big melting pot of around 50 cousins! It's a great mix.

My grandparents lived in Nigeria so they weren't around much, but we would go to visit them occasionally. I first went when I was five or six years old. It was surreal. Lagos is such a big, noisy city. I suppose it wasn't much different to London,

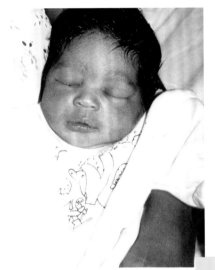

My mum was an immigrant from Nigeria and did so well for herself, I guess that's why I worked hard.

Our home was
pretty much an
open house, the door was
        literally wide open.

but the culture is completely different. Those trips were so exciting. I'd never want to go home. Most of the family in England got together as often as possible: birthdays, summer holidays, Christmas. My family love any excuse for a party! My cousins Ozzy, Immanuel and Moses lived in Wembley, north-west London and even though they were only 45 minutes away, whenever we went to visit it felt like the car journey lasted about five hours. I'd always fall asleep on the back seat and wake up to find we were still on the road. Eventually though, when we finally made it, I'd soon find enough energy to race around the house with my cousins. I loved it there and we'd stay for like three weeks out of the summer holidays to give my parents a break. All the kids would play together all day, every day, while the grown-ups caught up. They are some of my most magical memories.

I was quite creative as a kid and I used to draw a lot. My favourite thing to draw was Sonic the Hedgehog and Dragon Ball Z characters. I even made up my own character called Coach Squirrel – I could still probably draw him now if I tried. I think I was inspired by the film *Space Jam* – I also had DJ Quack Quack who was a duck!

Me and my brother and sisters all got on amazing as kids. I was very aware I was the oldest and I acted like it too! I used to tell the others to do such bad things. One day I remember turning to them all in Kelly's room and going, 'Let's draw stuff on the wall, let's just do it.' So, we're there, drawing on the wall, when I hear my mum coming into the house. So, I'm like, 'Guys, I'll be back in a minute.' Then I put my pen down and ran out of the room. Next thing, my mum comes upstairs and she catches my sisters in Picasso mode and goes really mad! They tried to blame me, but I was innocent until proven guilty. We kids were all really close and still are. I'd do anything for them. And I'm a much nicer big brother these days. A bit nicer, anyway.

When I look back on those days, I think about how naïve we all were really. The Aylesbury Estate was our whole world. Apart from those rare trips to Nigeria and those loooong trips to Wembley, we were rarely out of Peckham. First, we lived in a big tower block, then we lived in a maisonette nearby. It was the end house on the second floor, No. 46, and there was a pub right next door. I'll never forget the

Doberman that used to walk around in the pub garden. We weren't allowed to have pets so we would throw it food, like bits of meat from my mum's cooking pot, which meant he soon became sort of like our pet too.

One of the other figures in my life was our crazy uncle – Uncle Kenny. He's the man I talk about in 'Wonderman': 'My uncle used to drink a can of Kestrel when life got stressful.' He wasn't my actual uncle, but he was a friend of the family and a really nice guy. He was always at our house and Uncle Micah too. Uncle Micah was a friend of the family as well. Unlike most people we knew in our area, he was a university degree holder, but couldn't get a job. He'd get so frustrated. He was a trained mechanic, so he used to help my mum fix her car. But, every time my mum would short-change him, he'd be like, 'Listen, my sister! I'm a graduate in this country, I went to university!'

Our home was pretty much an open house – the door was literally always wide open. My mum would always be cooking and there was always more than enough just in case someone popped in. It was Nigerian food, like Jollof rice, which is basically like a risotto – rice in a yummy tomato sauce. We'd have a lot of black-eyed beans, with vegetables, beef, fish and chicken, too. Mum would always make us spicy chicken and there was a routine that she'd get us all involved in. We'd put curry powder in it, then thyme and a spice called All Seasoning. Then we'd leave it to marinate.

In between our cooking sessions, we'd hang out at my dad's barber shop. Sometimes Dad would ask us to help out, like tidy up, wash things down. I always used to moan, so Dad would just give me more and more chores. Like I said in 'Snap', that's when he got his first grey hair.

After a while my dad decided to give up the shop. In fact he and Mum decided to leave the area completely. Because Peckham was such a contained community, people started gossiping. It seems that trying to do well for yourself doesn't always go down that well. We were seen to be trying to do better and get out of the hood. People would be like, 'Who do they think they are? They've got their barber shop, it's not even doing that well.' But that wasn't the only reason Mum and Dad wanted to get out.

"HIGH RISES CAN LIMIT YOUR HORIZON."

Basically what happened was one of our neighbours got killed. I used to see this guy around, he was an older guy, well dressed, probably in his twenties – and then one day there were flowers by the bins. 'What happened?' I asked my mum. She looked down at me. 'He got killed. He was seeing a girl and she had another boyfriend, and the boyfriend got jealous and stabbed him,' she explained. 'We have to get out of here; I don't want you growing up in all of this.'

I didn't really understand it at the time. It was only when I got older and heard about people I'd known all my life getting shot and stabbed that I realised how precious life is, and how easily it can be taken away. I'm so thankful that I never got involved in that side of life; it's all so pointless and stupid.

Growing up on an estate is hard though, you see such a limited side of life. Like I said in 'Simply Unstoppable', about how 'high rises can block your horizon' – I meant that literally and metaphorically. Some people hardly ever leave their estate; they don't see there's a whole world of opportunity out there. It was for all of these reasons that my mum and dad moved us from Peckham to the more suburban area of Plumstead, south-east London, when I was 12. It was probably a good thing too, because the older I got the more rebellious I got...

School Days

My first school was St Francis Catholic School in Peckham. When we first started, my dad used to walk me and my sisters to the school gates. But by the time I was in Year 4, we'd walk to school by ourselves or our dad would take us to a certain point and then leave me and my sisters to it. We used to hold hands and go the rest of the way together. Imagine little me, holding my sisters' hands!

When we got to school we'd have a teacher at the gate waiting for everybody to come in. And, one day my teacher goes, 'Patrick, your shoes are on the wrong way round.' I looked down and my left shoe was on my right foot and vice versa. I just started crying, before turning around and running all the way home. I left my sisters there and ran – not so easy to do when your shoes are on the wrong feet! But I was so embarrassed.

I had my two 'rivals' at school. Philip – rest his soul, he was shot and killed when we were about 20 – and Sanchez, who I still see once in a while. They were real popular at school and I always used to try and be around them. Sometimes they'd make fun of me, but other times we'd be really good friends and walk home together. It was weird.

On the whole though, I was pretty much well behaved. My parents were very strict about school, so I just got it done. My mum was an immigrant from Nigeria and did well for herself. She used to work in the clothing trade, so she'd go to Switzerland or America and buy clothes and sell them wholesale back in England. I guess that's why I worked hard at school, my mum being such a workaholic.

When I got to Year 6, it was time for me to move to St Patrick's RC Primary School in Plumstead. I remember walking into St Patrick's and I was one of only two black kids. I was so used to being around black kids and now there were probably only ten in the whole school, if that. Anyway, I was late for my first lesson and when I walked in they were already doing maths. So I sat down and the teacher went, 'Can anybody tell me what six times seven is?' or whatever. No one put up their hand, so I put up my hand for every question and... I got every question right. I remember my first initial thought was, *What kind of place have I moved to?* My teacher though, Miss Linehan, she was lovely.

But there were definitely some new things I learnt about at St Patrick's. My first experience of kiss chase was when someone came up to me and said, 'Have you ever copped a girl before?' I was like, 'Huh? Er, yeah, yeah, of course I have.' So, I started running around with everybody but I had to keep looking at what the other lads were doing. I didn't have the first clue about what copping a girl was! I noticed that they were running after a girl, grabbing her and then the girl would stop and they'd kiss her – on the lips! There was this girl called Natasha and I remember I chased her as fast as I could, then I stopped her and... I kissed her. That was my very first kissing experience. I think we might have even done tongues and everything!

Discovering Music

For senior school, I went to St Paul's in Abbey Wood. At that stage, I guess I was thinking I'd probably be a lawyer or an accountant. One of my uncles was into fixing computers. I remember we bought a computer off him that he had made himself and I was amazed. *Wow, I wanna fix computers*, I thought. After a while I was like a fanatic about hardware; I'd break stuff up to put it back together without manuals and stuff.

The computer came in handy for helping me enjoy another passion: music. I've always loved music; my earliest recollection of it was the song on the advert for Vitalite margarine. I was just a little kid at the time, like three or four, and that was my favourite song. I used to jump up and dance to it every time.

I grew up on a lot of Dolly Parton, believe it or not. My mum loves her so I went to see her in concert and everything. Dolly Parton, I was on that! And then I listened to all the average stuff a young kid would listen to, from Britney to Busta and Tupac.

I first realised I wanted to make music myself when I saw the video to So Solid Crew's '21 Seconds'. I wanted to be in So Solid, I even started up my own crew and tried to be like them.

When I was about 14, I heard that Oxide & Neutrino, who were in So Solid, were shooting a video for their single 'Rap Dis'. They shot it in Greenwich Hospital, so I proper camped out till I got all of their autographs.

Inspired, it wasn't long after that I came up with my own stage name. I'm sure everyone's heard the story by now, but I got my name when I was in Year 8, in citizenship class. I was flicking through a thesaurus, daydreaming, and thinking of what I could have as a name. I didn't get very far – I only got up to 'A'! I saw 'angry' and beneath it the word 'temper' stood out, but I was aware that might sound a bit aggressive, a bit too much, so I randomly stuck 'tiny' at the front. By playtime I was Tinie Tempah and that's what I've been called ever since.

With my name established, I had a crack at writing my first lyric too. I befriended this guy called Sean Hobbs at school. He was like, 'I'm listening to this crew' and lent me all these tapes; this was the first time I heard real underground music – just people rapping over instrumentals on pirate radio. It was all really rough and informal, 'One two, one two, check, check, yeah, big up Nancy and Chanel on the Phoneline, gimme one missed call if you wanna hear that again... ' I became obsessed with pirate radio and started borrowing loads of tapes. They weren't big MCs, but after a while those tapes turned into Sharky Major and D Double E tapes, who were the main MCs back then.

I started listening to this one pirate station, Déjà Vu, and I heard Dizzee Rascal and that was it. Dizzee is still a major idol to me. The way he rapped, and what he rapped about, was so real. What I loved about Dizzee is that he was so uncompromising: he said what he wanted to and he said it how he wanted to. To me, that was so inspiring. That's when I started MCing. I wanted to be Dizzee Rascal! I used to write lyrics, memorise them, get home, type them up on my computer and then, next day, go to school to perform them. Everyone used to crowd round in a circle and I'd spit. I felt like a little superstar for a while – even though it was only 10 kids in my class who were watching! But it gave me a taste for performing and from then on I didn't want to do anything else.

The first rap I wrote is so bad though. It's stupid. Most of it didn't even make sense!

Girls go so low/ I'm a maestro/ Blazing a zoot/ Still hit a high note/ Never cause beef, beef stay on the low/ My crew too much, never solo/ Burberry/ Iceberg or Moschino (You can tell this is old!)*/ I'm a make a chick get on two knees and then blow/ Keep it quiet on a downlow* (Oh no, this is bad)*/ It's a me and you ting no one's gonna know.'*

Oh God, I told you it was bad! Luckily, the more I did it, the better I got. I'm not half bad now as it goes!

During these formative years, my cousin Henry became one of my best friends. We're the same age and he's an actor now, studies at RADA. He's really, really talented. We first properly met at my granddad's funeral in Nigeria around Year 8.

It was in this really dark long tunnel, the queue was all the way from the middle to the end of the tunnel. It was crazy, full of loads of people.

All the girls were like winding and stuff, and me and my little cousin were proper scared. 'What the hell?' That was my first experience of a grime rave.

I remember getting to Nigeria, and I saw this really cool, good-looking kid wearing a Man United top. I looked at my mum. 'Who's that?' I asked. 'That's your cousin Henry,' she replied. Me and Henry were chums straight away. At the end of our three- or four-week stay, we were both crying when it came to leave. So, back home in London, we started hanging out. From Year 9, he started staying at my house now and then, and that's when we started sneaking out to Eskimo Dance.

Eskimo Dance was in a tunnel in south-east London, in Elephant and Castle. We'd get the No. 53 bus and it would take us near enough there. It was in this really dark, long tunnel. It was crazy, full of loads of people and, to begin with, me and my little cousin were proper scared. That was my first experience of a grime rave.

We were obviously way too young to be there. Let's just say we didn't get in in the most orthodox way! Someone just buss the doors down and everyone ran in and the security guards couldn't really do anything. Once we were in I remember seeing Ghetto – he was like a superstar to me – Lethal Bizzle, Wiley and Sharky Major. All of my heroes. It was just the most amazing experience.

It was a Saturday night, and me and Henry had left pillows inside our duvets, Macaulay Culkin-style, before sneaking out. But we ended up getting back way too late. By the time we got home, my mum and dad were getting ready for church. Our house had this little outhouse behind it; me and Henry used to call it 'the house away from the house'. It was like a little side building and it had two rooms in it, a shower and stuff. My mum basically built it so we could have more space. 'Let's just go hide in the house away from the house,' I whispered to Henry. We were just about to sneak inside when my mum walked out in her church clothes. She looked sooo angry. 'When I get back...' she said, shaking her head. I got a few licks, I won't lie. And, trust me, we never ever did that again!

But that's when I realised I really, really wanted to do music. Seeing all my heroes, sneaking out to raves, listening to tapes of pirate radio and writing my own raps... it was all so exciting. In fact, I couldn't imagine doing anything else. I had to be a rapper, whatever it took.

Chapter Two:

MAKING IT HAPPEN

> "BEFORE I REACHED MY GOAL LOADS OF PEOPLE HAD TO BE TACKLED."

2:18 / 3:33

360p

Finding My Place

I never expected to be taken seriously when I first got into MCing. Back in 2005/2006, it was very much an east London thing; if you weren't from Bow, Limehouse or Newham, then people didn't really want to know. For me, it all stemmed from MSN. Everyone was on MSN: D-Dark, Royal, Ironik, and Chipmunk. People would talk through MSN and send tunes to each other to see what they had to say. So off the back of chatting to these guys, I found myself doing a few tracks with them and hanging out in the studio a bit. They were all involved in pirate radio and they'd all be like, 'Yeah, come on the radio with us.' Before you know it, I was on Axe FM, Hav It FM, Raw Mission FM and Blaze 99.9 FM, staying out way past the time I'd said I'd be home.

Around this time I started doing my GCSEs. Somehow, I managed to perfectly balance both school and music because MCing was still very much a hobby. I'd go to the radio sessions once in a while, spit a couple of bars, disappear for a few weeks, then come back again. This crew, Highly Rated, would come on after me sometimes and after a while I became friends with D-Dark, one of the members from the crew. He told me Aftershock were looking to start a new thing and wanted me to be part of it. 'We're gonna go meet Bruza,' he said one day. Bruza was so big back then. So even when he goes to me, 'All right, yeah?' I was beyond excited. Starstruck. Shortly after that we all started hanging around Forest Gate together. Terror Danjah, Magnum and another producer DOK all used to live on the same road, so we'd dip in and out of their houses listening to different beats.

It was around that time I made my first big song 'Wifey' with this producer called Flukes. We put it together in my friend's little studio, sent it round MSN and it suddenly blew up. All my friends on MSN were like, 'This song is huge. You should shoot a video for it and put it on Channel U.' Channel U was this independent TV channel where all the grime artists and MCs would post their videos. I spoke to Terror. 'I'm gonna do a video, but it's like a college project so it's nothing major,' I said. Terror didn't mind and even let me re-vocal it in his studio. Afterwards, I just

Suddenly, it was just me and Dumi just rolling. It was the start of a beautiful friendship!

FROM THIS DAY FORWARD MY LIFE MIGHT NEVER BE THE SAME AGAIN.

needed to plan the video, but videos cost money, so there was only one thing for it... I got a job doing double glazing telesales. It wasn't as boring as it sounds. I was quite good at it and the office was full of young kids, so the majority of the time we'd just doss about. There was a McDonald's right opposite, so we would be in there all the time too! But I always got the meal deals cos I needed to save.

After a while I managed to get the £800 I needed together. I'll never forget handing that money over to Carly Cussen and Digital Dan, who directed the video. £800! I'd never had that amount of money in my life and I swear it was all made up of small notes and coins. I was like, 'Right, £800, there you go, let's do the video. I want a car crash in it, I want to drive a nice car, I want to walk out of a big house...' They looked at me in amazement. 'We can't do that with £800!' But, you know what, we did. The song became massive and was at No.1 on the Channel U charts for 10 weeks.

Because I was from south London and not born in that east London world, where everyone at the time was completely engulfed in grime, grime, grime, I was still being influenced by loads of other styles of music around me; I was a sucker for a good-quality 'cheesy' pop song. So I was always persuading people to let me MC over their tracks with the intention of making a good 'pop' song out of it. Everyone thought I was different. But there was a particular group of people who loved my style – the girls! They'd turn up in flocks to watch me perform my music in small clubs in and around London. Before I knew it, I found myself on the same bills as Wiley, Boy Better Know and all the most credible MCs around. But still a lot of guys didn't like me. They'd all look at me funny, like, 'Who are you? Where did you even come from?' I just didn't fit in.

God, I remember teaming up with Bashy to do his 'Black Boys' (Remix). That was the most awkward day of my life! Bashy's always been a really good guy, and his tune 'Black Boys' was getting really big. He was like, 'I want you to do the remix, I'm getting loads of artists together.' So I went down to the studio. Skepta was there in African attire. Wretch 32 was there. Ghetto. No one said hello to me. No one spoke to me apart from maybe Skepta, Bashy and Chipmunk. We did a group photo, and bless

him, he's my good friend now, but when I went to stand on the end next to Wretch, he just moved all the way round to the other side! But it's all part of it. That's why I am the way I am, because I had a lot to get through. I had to find a way to be accepted.

The next big blow was when 'Black Boys' (Remix) went on MTV Base, which was a massive thing because nothing had been on proper TV before, just Channel U. But when the remix came on, it had everyone's name on it apart from mine. I was just like, *Boy...* It was a weird time. I said to myself, *You either have to stomach this and get through it, or just give up because they don't like you.*

While I tried to make my mind up, I carried on doing what I was doing. 'Wifey' made it on TV too and I started getting £200–£400 to do a show. I was 17 years old and performing at clubs for over-18s in front of loads of girls. I thought I was made!

Going It Alone

Then one day my mum made me go to this family gathering in a place called North Cheam, near Sutton. My mum spotted one of my many cousins and nudged me in my ribs. 'Talk to your cousin, you both do music,' she said. Despite being related, I'd never met Dumi before. Our family was so big, I had a lot of cousins like that and he was six years older than me, too. Dumi was looking to seriously get into music and knew a few people. Our mums were like, 'Oh, you two should definitely talk.' So we did what every dutiful son would do and made small talk. 'I've heard "Wifey", well done, it's good,' Dumi said. 'Thanks,' I said, but didn't really entertain the rest of the conversation. I was texting my boy Jaz, 'Come and pick me up from this place!' Jaz turns up in his Peugeot 206 and I'm like, 'Yes, let's go back to the ends!' I feel like I was a bit rude now. I just left and pretty much forgot all about my encounter with my cousin Dumi really.

Then three weeks later, me and Henry were walking out of the Odeon cinema in Greenwich when I noticed this big black guy get up from his table in the nearby Nando's. He came up to me and he's like, 'T! T! Do you remember me? I'm your cousin, bruv.' Dumi's wearing this sick leather jacket and Rolex. Then, he goes into his car, a

BMW Compact, and says, 'Take my number, let's chill.' I was quite impressed and we did end up chilling. He started coming to my house, or sometimes we'd just sit in his car and talk. I'd play him some of my tracks. He bought me a Samsung phone and some new trainers. So I was like, *Okay cool, this guy's a G*. He would pick me up outside my college, St Francis Xavier Sixth Form, and he'd take me to Nando's, five pounds on a Nando's meal. I was taken aback, like, *Whoa, I'm moving up in the world!*

Basically after our 'schmoozing' period, he said, 'T, I wanna manage you.' I was like, 'Okay, cool.' From then on, we were rarely apart. Although Dumi was now officially my 'manager', he was really laid back.

I was still kind of in Aftershock though, which was a bit of a problem. 'Listen, if I'm going to manage you, you have to leave Aftershock and you have to tell them because I know you're gonna be a big star,' Dumi said. 'I don't want you to have any grey areas where people will think you owe them.' So, I thought about it, spoke to Terror and we amicably parted company. Suddenly, it was just me and Dumi just rolling. It was the start of a beautiful friendship. You have to be able to see good in other people and that's why I think me and D got on so well, because I could see some of the qualities I had in him. Dumi's a nice guy, he listens, he's helpful, and he looks after me. Plus, there was the whole family thing. If you're going to get into this wicked world that is the music industry, you need somebody who you know has 100 per cent got your back at all times.

Dumi linked up with his close friend and business partner Lyndon and they both co-managed the project. Both had never done management on a professional level so we all learnt things as we went along. We spent lots of money on videos because we all believed in making a product to major record label standard. When we did 'Tears', Dumi was like, 'We're gonna spend £7,000 on this video.' I almost fainted. Seven grand! 'Tears' was A-listed on Radio 1Xtra and we ended up going on a few school tours off the back of it. We did this thing called Club D TV, which consisted of doing under-18 shows in super clubs all over England. Ironik was my DJ back then and I loved seeing all these new towns that I never knew existed.

But those early shows could be disheartening at times. I remember we drove all the way to Peterborough and no one was there. There were literally about 12 people, it was so empty. But the promoter told me I had to do the show, so I performed in front of those 12 people. I learnt a great lesson though: if you're gonna make it, you have to let go of all your insecurities and inhibitions.

Somehow in among all that, I still managed to do my A levels. I did Psychology, Religious Education and Media. I passed too! When I'd started them I'd been thinking about going to university and doing Media Studies. But by the end of my two years, my interest in it had gone. My parents weren't happy with the fact that I chose music over further education and there was a lot of tension in my house around that time. But that's when I became a full-time MC. It was probably the biggest step I ever took, but the best one too.

Spreading The Word

My first real offering after my big decision was 'Hood Economics Room 147 (The 80 Minute Course)'. It was mad creative! I had Chris Rock skits on there, anything that I thought was fun, whether it was controversial, cheesy, plain odd... I tried anything and everything. It was just me, rapping over whatever I wanted to. But because a lot of the MCs weren't accepting me into the grime scene, I did a few harder tracks too, so they could finally see I could MC and spit!

We made 10,000 copies of 'Hood Economics' because that's how confident we were with it. We went to see a distributor who would help us get our record into the shops. His name was Richard England and he ran a company called Cadiz Music. Richard said he'd help us distribute our CD, but we'd need to set up a record label. Dumi and Lyndon raced into action. They pooled every penny they had and set up a little office in a business complex in Greenwich. We called our label Disturbing London, because that's what we intended to do – to well and truly disturb London! Or wherever we went really.

About two months after releasing 'Hood Economics' we got an email from the *New York Times* asking for a picture of me. We didn't believe it, so we didn't send anything, and then a few days later there was this whole article on the intricacies of my lyrics and my flow. I was amazed. We realised we had to start taking things seriously. Very seriously.

I got back into the studio and started making more music. I was put under a very strict regime where I studied the music more and learnt about the proper way to mix tunes. When your song is played on the radio next to, say, Kanye West, it has to sound as good. For so long I'd been relying on other people to look after my music, but now it was incredibly important to be in control too. I wanted to be a professional. All you need is a good ear.

I really looked at my predecessors and how they marketed their albums, the videos they'd done. I analysed everybody. I was really very obsessed with it and soon had lots of ideas.

In January 2009, Dumi went to MIDEM, which is a music industry conference that happens every year in Cannes. He came back a new man. 'Tinie, Tinie, Tinie, it's all about the Internet,' he told me excitedly. So I set up my own blog. For the name, I started thinking about the things I love most. *I like tea*, I thought. *And I have it with milk and two sugars*. Milkand2sugars.com was born.

I've always had belief in myself, always been confident in my musical capability and talent. But for some reason all these other guys got signed before me: Chipmunk, Mr. Hudson – even my DJ [Ironik]! I hope Dumi doesn't mind me saying this, but he had to go back to his parents' house for a while. Because we'd put 100 per cent into what we were doing, we had to live a minimalistic lifestyle. Instead of getting better, things were getting harder. I got pretty low for a little while.

During those hard days, I used to get quite angry at times. I wrote this mixtape 'Sexy Beast' to help me vent some of my anger. I realise now I was just ignorant, bitter and jealous. But I couldn't help it. It felt like I was working so hard, but getting nothing in return. I even thought about giving up a couple of times.

When 'Sexy Beast' came out, I rang up Dumi. 'D, everyone has got record deals, am I not that good? Am I not making the right things? What's happening?' Dumi was like, 'Don't worry, all will be well bro, all will be well.' But then he said something that has stayed with me forever: 'You've been too complacent, T, you've not worked as hard as you could have. You haven't made as many mixtapes as you could have. You are talented, but we need to do more.' I realised he was right. You can never work too hard.

Slowly, things started to pick up. My blog got bigger and bigger and when I wasn't blogging, I'd be in the studio with these guys called All About She. I wound up in Jay Sean's video for 'Down' and we did a song called 'Still Love You', which got leaked. But on the whole, I just made sure I kept on top of my Internet game, uploading new tracks, videos, blogging... and it paid off. The word was getting out there and soon the record labels started sniffing around...

The Big Deal

I first did Wireless Festival in 2008 and I was only on a very small stage. But Steve Homer (who organises Wireless) saw something in me. He was like, 'I'm going to give you a chance.' And a year later, I was back at Wireless, but this time I had a really good spot, opening up the second stage and... it was absolutely rammed. In the crowd, there were some talent scouts. These A&R guys, as they call them in the music industry, were like, 'Who is this kid?' That was a key moment.

Not long after, I had a whole string of record labels asking for meetings: Atlantic, Ministry, Mercury, they all wanted to meet up. But there was only one label I could see myself with: EMI. It was for such simple reasons, too. Nathan Thompson, the A&R from the label, was a brutally honest guy. He told me the tracks he liked, the tracks he didn't like and what his vision was. Also Miles Leonard, the president of the label, came down to our studio in Greenwich. He got in a car and came all the way down there to ask me if I wanted a deal. No one else did that.

Finally, I had my own record deal. The feeling was incredible; I was the happiest guy on earth that day. I decided I wanted to do a competition to sign the deal at a fan's house, because the fans had been such a huge part of my journey. We had hundreds and hundreds of kids enter, and I picked this girl, Tia, from Manchester, because she came up with the right answer. The question was: 'Why should I sign my deal at your house?' and she said: 'It's not just about your music, it's about the whole scene. I believe in the scene and I want it to become like America.' She got it.

Sadly, because of all the health and safety aspects, we had to change the prize a bit. Parlophone, which is the division of EMI I am with, said, 'Seeing as you like tea so much, there's this place called Claridge's where you can have afternoon tea. It's really posh and fancy.'

I vividly remember us leaving Dumi's house to go to Claridge's. It was a really sunny day and Dumi started singing Bob Marley's 'Sun Is Shining'. We were walking along, our shades on and all I could think was, *Oh my God, this is actually happening. From this day forward my life might never be the same again*. It was a wicked moment.

So, over afternoon tea with one of my greatest fans, I signed a record deal and not just any record deal. I joined a great roster of British talent: Lily Allen, Gorillaz, Coldplay... It was like the equivalent of getting that degree my mum had wanted me to get. I got the label to make me up one of those life-sized cheques so I could put it on my mum's wall. She might not have a picture of me in a cap and gown, but that deal meant the world to me. It's what it represents. I didn't care about fame. Signing to a label, getting to No.1, it wasn't about that. The thing that made me proud is that I had a vision, it's all I thought about for years, and I made it happen. And I made it happen in the biggest way possible.

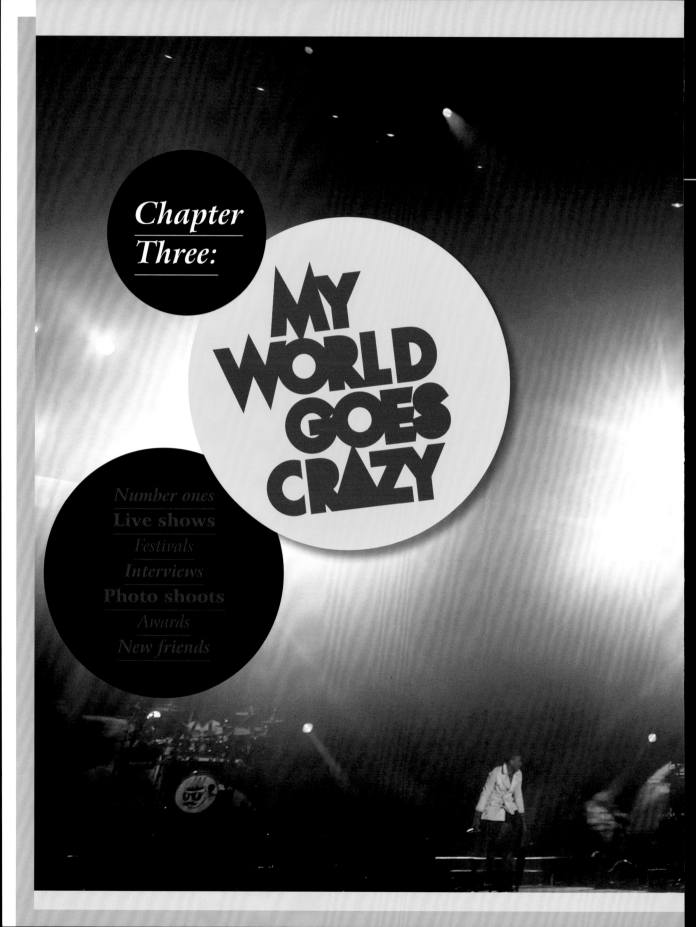

Chapter Three:

MY WORLD GOES CRAZY

"I'm about to be a bigger star than my mum thought."

After finally signing my deal, that was when the real hard work began. Don't get me wrong, I'd been working hard before then, but signing to EMI meant I had one shot to get it right. Really, really right. So I spent a lot of time in the studio, but outside the studio my world went really crazy, really quickly. It's all a bit of blur, but it felt like before the ink had even dried on the contract, I was supporting some of the biggest names in music, winning awards, getting my first number one, and all the other things I'd never thought about… like my name all over the newspapers and my face on TV. I'd waited years for something to happen and then when it did, it all happened so very quickly. It's been one hell of a ride and I've made some amazing friends along the way.

Number One

Things really started to go mad when I got my first No.1 with 'Pass Out'. And for that, I've got to pay a lot of thanks to Labrinth. I first heard about Labrinth through Master Shortie's album, *A.D.H.D.*, which came out in July 2009. I thought the album was amazing and very advanced for its time. I was like, *Who made that? Who's singing on that?* It turned out that 90 per cent of it was a guy called Labrinth. The way his beats and voice sounded, I thought it was going to be some 30-year-old white guy. When I got the opportunity to have a session in the studio with him, I still didn't know what he looked like. I got to his studio in north London and I'm like, 'I've got a session with Labrinth' and there's this really young black guy staring at me. Eventually it clicked. *Oh, this is Labrinth.* We got talking about our upbringings and us both coming from big families; he's got nine brothers and sisters like my mum.

Lab is amazing. He's a genius. He's so talented, so hard-working. I've never seen anybody make as many instruments out of their body as him. So many of the noises you hear on 'Pass Out' are from Lab's mouth or body, not a machine or sample! You stand there watching him thinking, *What the hell? This guy is a nutter.* He was the first producer who made me feel comfortable in the studio. He's like a big kid and I'm like a big kid, too. He created the coolest environment to create music in. He is, simply put, a genius.

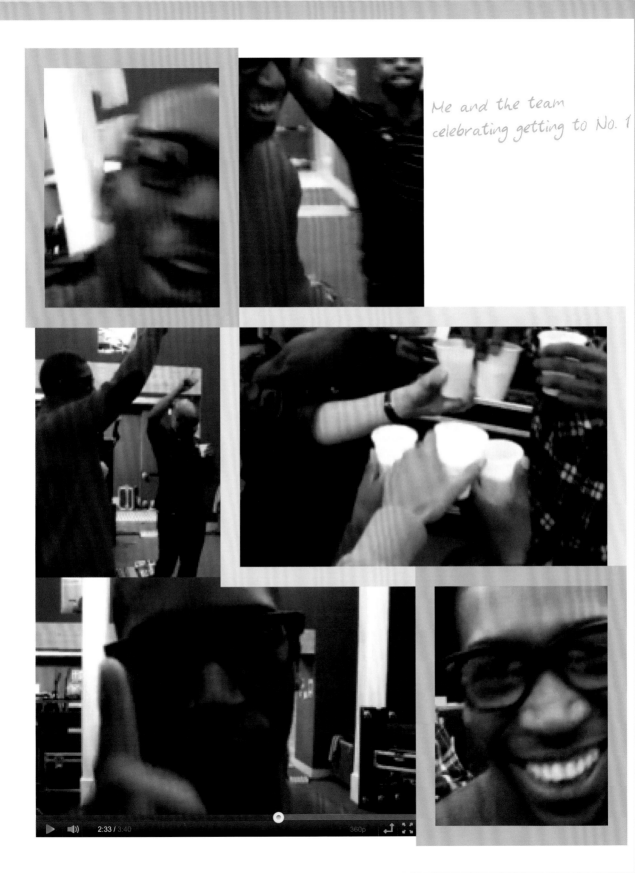

Me and the team celebrating getting to No. 1

In between laughing and joking, Labrinth started playing some beats and I was like, 'Do you know what, Lab? This is my situation. I've just been signed and I'm feeling like sod the rules, I'm feeling mad confident. I want to do something so different. Something that me and you can listen to for the rest of our lives and always be proud of.' And he was like, 'Okay, one second.' And then all I hear is 'Do-do-do-do-do-do...' You know the bit I mean, right at the beginning of 'Pass Out'. I looked at Dumi and he was like, 'Yeah, yeah, yeah!' Then Marc Williams, Lab's manager, started jumping around, swinging his dreads everywhere! I was like 'Yeah, this is the one. This is the one!'

Next I tried to put some lyrics together. I started with 'Yeah, we brought the stars out, we brought the women and the cars and the cards out...' But it didn't sound quite right. So I was like, 'Lab, brought or bring?' Lab said, 'Try bring.' Straight away it sounded so much better.

I don't know where the words came from; I just said anything that came into my head. 'I never got to fly on a Concorde, I've been Southampton but I've never been to Scunthorpe...' By the end of it, it just sounded so wicked man, so wicked. Then Master Shortie walked in – normally I don't like people hearing my songs until they're finished – but Labrinth played it and Shortie looked blown away. 'This is sick,' he shouted.

By the end of the session, the song was finished, apart from the, 'So we let it rain' bridge bit. Labrinth had his two stylists there as well and when we played the song back, the girls were rapping everything, like 'In charge now...' I was standing in the middle of the studio and everything was just blurry. I swear, it was like a movie. I felt like something special was going to happen. And that's basically how 'Pass Out' happened.

I think there's a certain chemistry, like a Jay-Z and Kanye or Eminem and Dr. Dre partnership, with me and Lab. There's a musical magic that happens. When we get into the studio it's not about, 'Oh, what was that girl saying from last night', it's more, 'T, do that eight bars', 'Lab, do that hook'. By the end of the day there's a winning tune. When you find that chemistry with someone you stick to it. The first tune we made was 'Pass Out', and we did it in under 24 hours. So we just kept teaming up again and again. The next one we did was 'Wonderman', then 'Frisky'...

I think it was at the BRITs 2010 when I had an inkling that 'Pass Out' might become a really big deal. It wasn't due out for another month or so, but literally everybody, people I didn't think would even know me, came up to me to say hello: heads of labels, A&Rs, artists, everyone. They were all really excited about it and that was the most important thing. The track was uncompromising and it didn't feel diluted in any way, shape or form, we just wanted to make something amazing. I didn't think about radio, or what the papers might say or if I had too many swearwords... I really didn't think anything. It was one of the most unconventional tunes ever. It proper broke the mould of what an actual pop record is supposed to be like.

That was the first time I'd ever been to the BRITs. We were invited by this big artist agency, William Morris, so we could see what goes on at the event. I was wearing a black sequinned jacket with a grey T-shirt that had a zebra on it, some jeans and some sparkly Nike trainers. I ironed everything hours before I needed to go because I was so nervous and excited. A car came to get us and I remember pulling up at Earls Court and having to do the red carpet. I was behind Leona Lewis, and no one wanted to ask me any questions! Nobody! It was so nerve-racking. The agents were like, 'Do you guys wanna talk to Tinie?' And, you could see it in their eyes, the press were like, 'No, not really, but okay.' Just to be polite. In many ways that was the event that marked the calm before the storm.

On 7th March 2011 I got my very first No.1. The week before, on the Sunday night, I'd been in Sheffield supporting Chipmunk. At the stroke of midnight on the Monday morning, 'Pass Out' literally went straight to No.1 on iTunes. I was so excited I felt sick. I was walking around like I was in a trance. iTunes wasn't the official chart, but even so it was more than enough to be happy about. By the time we got to Chipmunk's after party it was 1 a.m. Chipmunk rushed up to me. He was like, 'Yeeeeeeeeah, you're No.1! We're going to celebrate.' Everyone was splashing each other with champagne, jumping up and down. That was the first time I've ever had champagne thrown at me and let me tell you, it stings! Luckily I had my glasses on!

The next day was the 'Pass Out' single launch at a club called the 229 in the West End, London. That was a big day because it was the first time my dad had seen me perform live, which was very special. By then, we were pretty sure it was going to be a No.1 because it was selling so strongly.

When I performed 'Pass Out' I remember looking out at all my family and friends who were literally jumping up and down and going mad. I felt so happy I actually could have burst! I was elated.

On the actual Sunday, we went on Radio 1's Chart Show, which is presented by Reggie Yates. We had a lot of tough competition out there that week too – Rihanna, Lady Gaga and Beyoncé all had singles out. So, even though sales had been strong, I was still scared.

So I get in there, Reggie's looking at me really excited. And I'm stepping on my toes anxiously and just jumping, jumping, jumping... He announced to me live on air, 'I can tell you the No.2 record is... Rihanna with "Rude Boy"!' Everyone went absolutely crazy, shouting, cheering, hugging... Dumi cried. It was beautiful; it was such a sick day. Afterwards we went to Côte on Wardour Street, Soho. We had a good steak, some wine and it was like, 'Yes lads, this is the beginning of a lot more amazing things.'

Afterwards we went to a club called 24 and everyone was there. Tinchy came down, Chipmunk, Roll Deep, Labrinth was there, Manny Norté was DJing and everybody was throwing me in the air. iSHi, who produced 'Written In The Stars' was congratulating me and I whispered in his ear, 'Don't worry, we're going to get our No.1 together soon and it's gonna be huge!'

I still lived at my parents' house then and I got home really late, about 5 or 6 a.m. I just lay down on my own and thought, *This is insane, this is crazy.* I literally felt like I was on top of the world at that point.

In the back of my mind though, I was thinking, *What next?* It was cool but people had got No.1's before. I knew I still had a lot to prove and I knew I still had a lot more to achieve.

Doing It Live

In my early days, I supported Chipmunk, Chase & Status and N-Dubz and had a wicked time on the road with all of those guys, so much fun. When Rihanna asked me to join her on her UK tour, I said yes, of course. Hell yes! Rihanna is amazing.

It's a really good experience being able to support talented people like Rihanna, Usher and The Black Eyed Peas. What's great is that they've enjoyed my set even as a warm-up act. I always deliver in that way. I've played big venues before, so I don't find that intimidating and whether I'm supporting or headlining, I always put 100 per cent effort in.

When Usher invited me on tour, we became really good friends. He's my bredrin. He's such a nice guy, flippin' hell. He watched my show a few times while we were making our way around Europe together. And, he was like, 'You're throwing it down man!' and I'm like, 'Really? Thanks Ush.' It was really hard to stay cool. It was Usher! Mr 'Yeah'! 'OMG'! 'Pop Ya Collar'!

Soon me and Usher were texting all the time! He'd be asking me how I was doing, how the album was doing, telling me that 'Frisky' was his favourite song off the album. I was talking about spending time with my family in one text and he replied, 'Yeah, family is very important.' Big boy texts.

Sometimes I sit back and just laugh at these kind of things. Life can be so strange sometimes. Amazing, but very odd!

It isn't just indoor shows you get to do – summertime is all about the festivals. I think one of my favourite early ones was when I did Radio 1's Big Weekend in Bangor. I had a ball onstage and I came off all sweaty, with my top off. I saw this guy in a baseball cap and his beautiful girlfriend, waiting for me. I looked under his cap and I froze. *I know that face!* They just looked like a very normal, happy couple – but it was the future King and Queen, Prince William and Kate Middleton. William was really dressed down. Kate looked gorgeous in a nice dress. He put his hand on my shoulder and I cringed. I was so sweaty, like *Eurgggh*. He made a little joke about

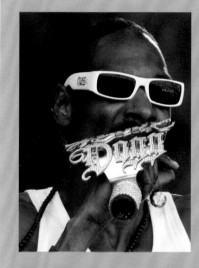

Snoop had this whole entourage, security guys in big suits, and then there was me, hiding in the corner. He said to me, 'So, we're gonna go out there after "Sexual Seduction"!'

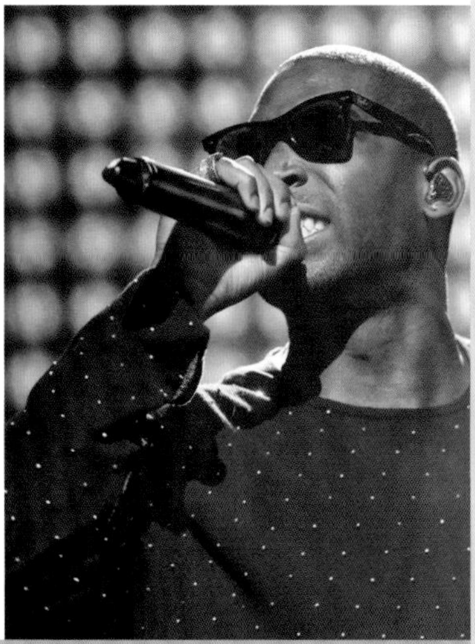
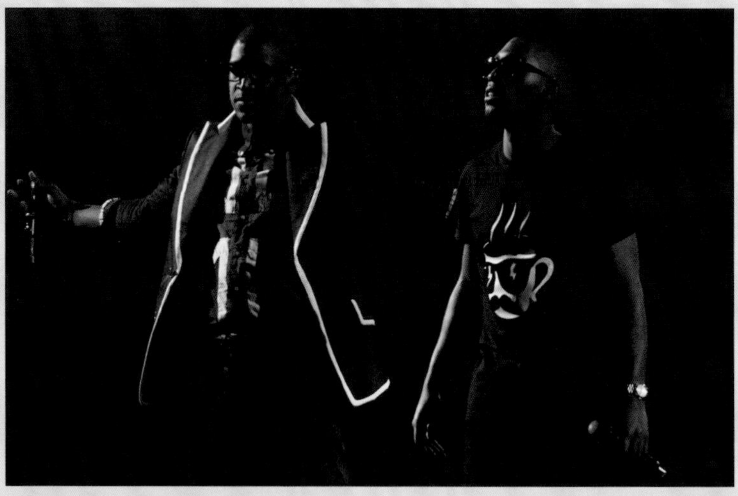
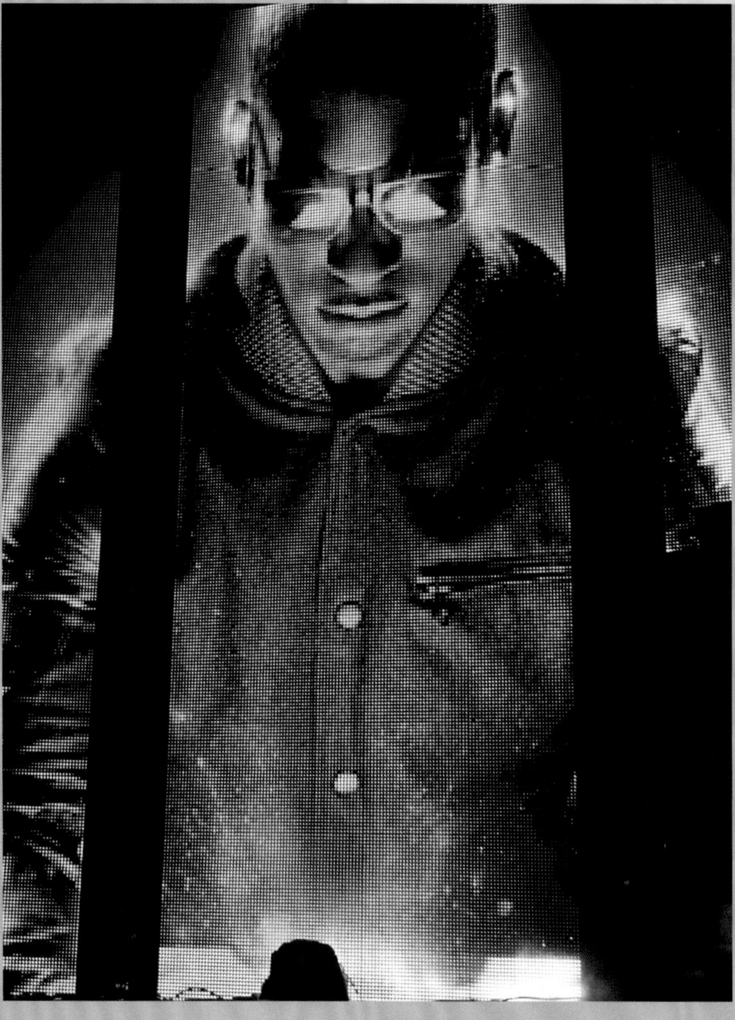
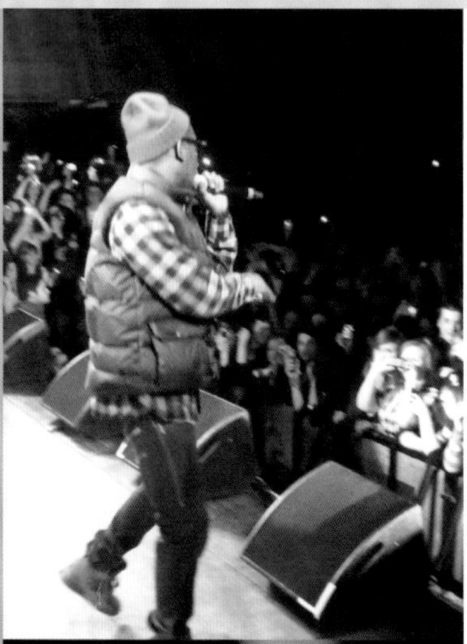
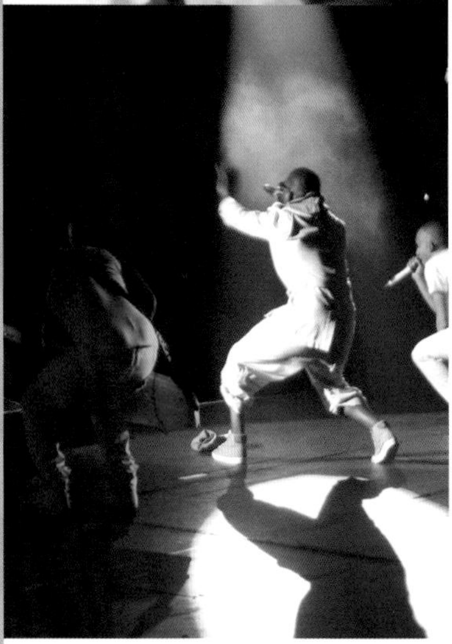

Performing live is
what it's all about,
especially with artists
like Lab and Ellie.

my trousers being so low, saying he thought they were going to fall off halfway through my performance and said he loves going to festivals but he goes incognito.

His servant, or whatever they are called, came out with a box of Soleros and there was only four in there, but there were five of us in the room. William offered me one and I was like, 'No thanks.' I didn't wanna deprive the future King of his Solero! By the time Ellie Goulding came off stage from her set, we were *still* talking. Ellie put her arms out to give me a hug, but I directed her hand towards William instead. I was like, 'You can't shake my hand before you shake his!' She went so white. A year later, she was playing at William and Kate's wedding reception. Pretty incredible stuff.

Of course, the mother of all festivals in Britain is Glastonbury. My first appearance there was one of 2010's biggest highlights for me. It was the first time I met Snoop Dogg. We were both on the line-up, but we were on different days, so I didn't think I'd get to meet him. But then on the way to Somerset, I realised we were a day early (you lose track of the days once your schedule goes crazy!). So, I started asking questions, but Dumi was really vague. When we got there, he stepped out of the car and grinned. 'So, Snoop wants to perform with you,' he revealed. My stomach flipped. I was like, 'No way! Sick!' Next thing, I'm being walked into Snoop's dressing room. He was sat in between a girl's legs, getting his hair braided. He looked so cool. I was so nervous I ended up finding myself standing by the water cooler. Snoop had this whole entourage, security guys in big suits, and then there was me, hiding in the corner. He said to me, 'So, we're gonna go out there after "Sexual Seduction",' and then he turned to his crew. 'Has anyone heard this guy's song before?' He whipped out his iPad and played 'Pass Out'. The band listened to the song twice and then... it was show time! While I waited at the side of the stage to go on, I paced up and down.

Then, I froze, I could hear him introducing me as 'My homie Tinie Tempah!' I was like, *Oh God!* I jumped onstage in whatever I was wearing when I arrived, shorts and a black tee. I have never felt that much adrenalin. It couldn't have lasted more than four minutes, but I remember halfway through I just looked at Snoop and thought, *Is this real?* I'm not sure anything will top that again.

THE TIMES

Max 12C, min 0C

Friday January 14 2011 | thetimes.co.uk | No 70156

PHIL KNOTT FOR EMI

Babies 'need olid food

th
all
breast-
European
d not follow the
Britain's change was
surprisingly little scrutiny"
from scientists, Professor Lucas said.

"I'm very pleased they are reviewing
it. At least now we will have a reasoned,
evidence-based decision," he said.

Fresh evidence has raised concerns
that babies fed purely on breast milk
for six months might not get the
Continued on page 8, col 4

their children s
onths, but a series of studies
t this could lead to long-term
the experts from London, Edin-
and Birmingham say.
r view as authors is that the most
le middle ground at present is
o six months," Alan Lucas, the
r of the Childhood Nutrition

The London rapper Tinie Tempah picked up four Brit nominations. News, page 4

It's written in the stars. Tinie leads way to Brits

Clegg ca immedia by-electi post mo

Anushka Asthana
Chief Political Correspond

Nick Clegg has ordered
post-mortem examinatio
election result in Oldhar
dleworth, asking his mini
at a meeting in London t

News of the talks, wh
just how high-stakes th
been for the Liberal Der
emerged last night as vo
the polls in the first ele
the new Westminster po

They were met by act
three main parties who
streets until late into
Some appeared to be ma
tations by warning that
become extremely close a
call. A senior Lib Dem s

Mr Invincible f blanks at bank
Ann Treneman, page 20

that even a defeat wou
result for the party, if the
not too large. A governing party
in this. A governing party
a seat in a by-election s
said. "Sometimes you ar
a gale that is just too stro

Elwyn Watkins, the
date, looked tired as h
streets knocking on do
polls closed at 10pm
happens I am proud of
done. There is no shame
what you believe in and le

Mr Watkins trigge
election by successfully c
Labour opponent in the
ion, Phil Woolas, in cour
in his favour, agreeing tha
won by only 103 votes,
Mr Watkins in his electio

THE NEWS

ious military row
rmer senior diplomat
sed the Army of sending
ps to fight and die in
anistan four years ago to
the Government from
cing its size as operations
q dried up. **News, page 3**

Cameron on tour
David Cameron is to release
himself from the shackles of
Whitehall and escape
Downing Street for visits to the
regions amid concerns that he
is spending too much time
behind his desk. **News, page 5**

Lies and subterfuge
An undercover officer who
worked for the police unit
co-ordinating the surveillance
of domestic extremists has
spoken out amid controversy
over his former colleague Mark
Kennedy. **News, pages 6, 7**

£20k a year to study
The accountancy firm KPMG
is offering to pay secondary
school leavers upwards of
£20,000 a year while they
study at university, in a
landmark scheme launched
yesterday. **Business, page 43**

Spurs eye windfall
Tottenham Hotspur expect to
earn at least £150 million from
selling the naming rights to a
new stadium in the Olympic
Park in East London after the
2012 London Games, *The
Times* has learnt. **Sport, page 88**

Front Page News

When you become famous, you have to get used to seeing yourself in the papers a lot. The question I get asked the most is 'How did you come up with your name?' and 'Do you enjoy doing collaborations?' You have to explain your story to those that don't know it, I get that.

As I got bigger though, I started getting more challenging questions and it became that British media 'thing' – more people trying to catch you out. I'm lucky in that I've always been quite media-savvy. People have asked me if I've been media trained but I haven't. I can weave my way in and out of tricky questions quite easily.

More recently there have been a few things I didn't like, like *Newsnight*. It was this patronising guy who just wanted to talk about some Tinie and Tinchy beef and stupid stuff like that. I was thinking to myself, *I haven't come here for this...* He was like, 'Do you guys have rap wars and beefs?' and I was like, 'Come on man, don't be that ignorant.' It was just the usual stereotypical rubbish.

The first time I got papped, it got really crazy. It was at the MOBOs 2010 in Liverpool. There was a guy waiting outside the hotel and he snapped a picture when we came out. The weird part was I then got into a cab and a motorbike started following it. It was in the papers next day, with details of where I went for dinner and all that. It was just mad to think people would really want to know that about me. I'm kind of used to it now though, seeing myself in the paper. The worst ones are like 'Tinie Tempah spotted with so-and-so female friend in Shoreditch House' or wherever. When you see that you think, *Someone was watching me and I didn't even see them watching me...* that's quite a weird feeling.

Thankfully, there haven't been many tabloid rumours about me. I was linked to DJ Yasmin and also Adele – that was stupid. And, have you heard the one that I'm moving to Sandbanks? I just said I liked it and the next thing I'm moving there! It's very lovely around there, but I've no plans to move there just yet!

The first couple of photo shoots you do are exciting but then at the same time when I was still new, I used to find it difficult to say to the stylist, 'I don't really like that.' I'll be honest: photo shoots have never really been the most exciting thing for me. It's a lot of waiting around, people trying to influence what you want to wear, you not wanting to always wear what they suggest, cos it's not your style. And then you have to stand about for ages pulling faces. Usually, I try and get some music playing really loud because that helps pass the time.

When it comes to the media, there have been moments over the last 18 months that have just been amazing. Moments that when they happen, you almost can't believe it. Being on the front of *The Times* was definitely one of them.

My bank manager called me at 7 a.m. He's an old Indian guy and he's usually only concerned about my money! He rang me, 'I'm in the office and everyone is talking about this cover from *The Times*!' I was like, 'What? The magazine?' And he said, 'No, the whole newspaper!' I got up, put on a tracksuit, came out of the flat and went into a corner shop. I picked up *The Times*, put it on the counter, quickly paid and then I put it in a plastic bag. I held that plastic bag so tight, but when I got home it went straight in a drawer at home. I shoved it in and closed it and I never read it. I don't really like reading press, but it was such a big deal that, one day, when I need inspiration or when I'm moving out of that house, I'll see it and it will give me that little boost I need.

For me, as a young, black rapper, it was a huge deal. Usually when you see a black person on the front cover of a newspaper, it's for something negative. Young people are misrepresented in the media, it's all ASBOs and hoodies. That's why it meant so much to me. It was a big day for rap, for black British music and for black kids in general. I hope that a lot of people kept that copy of *The Times* because not only was it significant for me, but for all black mothers and fathers out there. Without being patronising or clichéd, I feel like I was their child. It felt like I was a black son for all the black parents out there. Without a doubt that's been one of the most important, significant accomplishments of not just my career, but my life to date.

Lights, Camera, Action

I've had great support from the music channels, but now I've made appearances on lots of very different TV shows. Going on Graham Norton was a fun one. I think it showed more of my personality. I was really nervous beforehand. It's funny because I'd been in the same clothes all day and I felt disgusting. Right at the last minute, Dumi burst in with an overnight bag of fresh clothes – blazers, trainers and a shirt.

I was on there with Kate Hudson and the comedian Russell Kane. I was the underdog beside two big stars. But you know on shows like that when people are holding mugs and it looks like it's tea? Well, it's alcohol! So, I didn't mean to, but I ended up getting a bit drunk and I'm like, *I've gotta say something now…* So, I turned to Kate and I asked her quite a rude question. Everyone started laughing. Kate was blushing and suddenly, the whole show was revolving around me. It was a really transitional moment for me.

The X Factor is probably one of the biggest shows I've ever done. It's become a form of entertainment in its own right really, instead of a way to find new talent. But it does give people a chance to live out their dreams. I went to one of the live shows with Kelly Rowland. It was quite fun, and they said, 'Do you want to do one?' I was like, 'Yeah, all right then.' For the show, One Direction, Mary Byrne and Cher Lloyd met me backstage.

My TV highlight has to be Jools Holland. It was such an honour because it's all about the music. It really can make or break an artist. I was on with Two Door Cinema Club, Bryan Ferry and Jessie J. I remember Bryan Ferry's backing singers going crazy when I did 'Pass Out'. I bounced all over the studio, pushing my face into the camera. I was so hyped because he doesn't really have many rappers on his show, so I took it as a chance to show that we don't just mumble into a mic, grabbing our, well, you know what!

Jools has broken a lot of people like Adele and Amy Winehouse, God rest her soul, and so I was unbelievably happy to be there.

Behind the scenes at a recent photoshoot: usually, I try and get some music playing really loud because that helps pass the time.

My TV highlight has to be Jools Holland. It was such an honour because it's all about the music.

Awards

As I found my feet in the music industry and adapted to fame, it became clear that certain things you have to do are much more enjoyable than others. Picking up an award in recognition of your hard work is definitely one of them. It just seems to make everything worthwhile.

The MOBOs 2010 was very good to me. I was there to collect two awards for Best Newcomer and Best Video for 'Frisky' and I was performing too. It was amazing to see the best of British talent at that time all there to support one cause. Everyone was big in their own right, everyone got their own time, their own cheer and it was a beautiful thing.

When it came to the BRITs, I was high just off the nomination night! It was down at the 02 Arena in London and I performed 'Wonderman' with Ellie. I was high on getting four nominations. For a long time, a rapper like me would never have been invited. Not only that, but I was the most nominated artist! Everyone on the night only had good things to say and the lovely Fearne Cotton hosted it. They announced the nominations and I just kept hearing my name again and again: Best Newcomer, Best British Single, Best Album, Best Male. I was like, *Flippin' hell, this is sick. What's happening here?*

On 'Hood Economics' I say 'Gimme a few years/ Two MOBO's, a Brit and a VMA...' It all came to pass. But let me tell you something, they don't tell you what you're going to win. Honestly, I was hoping for Best Newcomer and Best British Single – and those were the ones I got. Best Newcomer was quite early on in the ceremony, so I just sat there, more nervous than I'd ever been in my life. I had butterflies, I hadn't eaten. I was so anxious, sat there in this smart suit. I felt weird, like groggy. But then, I realised everyone was shouting 'Tinie Tempah!' and I felt all these hands on me. It was all blurry, like being underwater and hearing someone calling your name. Dumi was like, 'You have to get up, bruv! You've won!' Someone helped me up, I can't remember who. I can't remember the speech at all. I hadn't written a speech or anything.

During the second award, Labrinth was in the toilet! I thought it would only make sense if I was there with Labs. I looked over at his manager Marc and he just mouths 'He's in the loo!' But when I did the Ivor Novellos, I made it up to Lab. I was like 'This one's all you mate', and let him do all the talking.

Anyway, when they said Best Single, I sort of knew I had it – Alan Carr gave it away. He was presenting the award and said something like, 'Oh my God, this is going to be like a flipping Specsavers commercial!'

Afterwards we went to the EMI after party on a boat and everyone wanted to come up and congratulate me. I had to thank absolutely everybody – everybody! By the time I got off the boat, I hadn't even taken one sip of my drink. It was crazy.

The response I got after winning my Brits was amazing. It was like people genuinely felt like they were a part of my success. People are still telling me that it was like England winning the World Cup. I was kinda like a People's Champion.

It's always nice to be acknowledged for something, whatever it is you do. It's always great for someone to pat you on the back and say, 'Well done, we've noticed this about you, we appreciate it and we're praising you for it.'

I'll never forget finding out I'd been nominated for the Mercury Prize – I heard from Adele! I thought my time was gone because it had been released in October 2010, and I said as much to Adele. 'Babe, you're going to be nominated, shut up,' she replied. Then one day she BBM'd before I even heard about the shortlist. 'What did I tell you? Congratulations,' she wrote, and then she put the BBM eyelash face. 'This is amazing. Who am I up against?' I asked. 'Me,' she replied with another eyelash face.

MOBOs, BRITs, Ivor Novellos, Mercury Prize, these are all award ceremonies I used to dream I'd end up at, but they all happened. It's so crazy, I'm not sure if I'll ever believe it's true.

Me and my mum and dad after the BRITs.

'Oh my God, this is going to be like a flipping Specsavers commercial!'

I realised everyone was shouting 'Tinie Tempah!' and I felt all these hands on me. It was all blurry, like being underwater and hearing someone calling your name. Dumi was like, 'You have to get up, bruv! You've won!'

MAKING NEW FRIENDS

Lily Allen

I met Lily at the BRITs the very first time I went in 2010. She's very normal, down to earth, and very easy to get on with. I wasn't invited to her wedding, but you never know, maybe I will if she renews her vows!

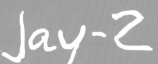

Adele

We met properly in LA when we both happened to be there. We'd already been emailing about music, so we went out for dinner. She's so comfortable in herself, a really open person and phenomenal talent. She's a wicked, wicked person.

Jay-Z

I first met Jay-Z at his concert in Manchester when I was supporting him. He was a true gentleman. I stopped him backstage and he looked me in the eye and went, 'My man!' and put his hand on my shoulder. That meant a lot to me.

Gwyneth Paltrow

I got invited to see a secret Beyoncé show and Gwyneth Paltrow was there. I was with my cousin Henry. So I said, 'Excuse me, Gwyneth, my cousin here is also an actor.' They started chatting. Afterwards, she tweeted about us, calling Henry my 'very handsome cousin'. It was so funny, he almost passed out!

Jessie J

She's a super cool girl — I have a lot of respect for her and I think she respects what I do as well. She's breaking the States at the moment like I am, so we see each other at random places all over the US.

Dizzee

I first met Dizzee at a party. He was standing next to this model, and I was like, 'All right Dizz?' He introduced us, 'This is Tinie Tempah, he's up and coming.' I couldn't believe he knew who I was! Now, he always makes time to hang out with me and Dumi.

Ellie and me first met outside Universal Records. We've been hanging out ever since and, of course, working together too, on 'Wonderman' and various shows. She's a really cool chick.

Sometimes, even if we're not performing together, we'll have a few drinks with her boyfriend Greg. She's so talented, I know she's going to be around for a long time to come. She's the best.

NEW FRIENDS MADE

JLS

'When he gets onstage he has the swagger of Jay-Z, it's electrifying. Then when you meet him offstage he's totally chilled out, like one of your family. He's going to be massive, a household name not only in America, but around the world.'

Example

'I think the secret to his success is that he's the only megastar I know who manages to be both aspirational and attainable at the same time. You can imagine people worshipping him like a God, but they also feel they could join him for a pint down the pub.'

Eliza Doolittle

'Tinie has always been the loveliest guy. I've never heard anybody say one bad thing about him. But it's Tinie's quirky lyrics and charisma that have done it for him. I am endlessly entertained by his backstage banter!'

Ellie Goulding

'I think the key to Tinie's success is his attitude and personality. He works hard, and he is grateful for everything that has happened to him. He's a genuine and lovely person with amazing style and intelligence. Love ya T!'

'When it came to getting the hottest UK rappers for the "Hello Good Morning" (remix) then of course we had to get Tinie. He has so much swag. I love the UK, the artists, the vibe, the style. I think we have an affiliation with each other.'

Diddy

Wiz Khalifa

'His flow is amazing. It's different, but there's nothing wrong with being different. Tinie has found a way to mesh everything and make everybody feel comfortable. Plus the girls love him – he's a pretty swagged-out individual.'

'I love Tinie. I saw him play at Coachella, he was great. He also played in LA, where I live. We were going to try and do something together but the scheduling didn't work out. Hopefully in the future though, I'd love to work with Tinie!'

Joe Jonas

Chipmunk

'We go way back, me and him. We made our first song together when I was 14 so it's like I know the journey. Some of you may just know him from "Pass Out", but the guy has worked so hard.'

Chapter Four:

THE ROAD TO DISC·OVERY

"This is the discovery, everything in front of me."

In the process of making an album you make loads of songs and sometimes one fits and it goes on to inspire the rest of the album. 'Pass Out' was that song.

It had worldwide appeal and it was messing with genres and twisting things up. So, that's what I did on the album - made songs longer or shorter than they should be or stopped them at weird points. Every idea I had before 'Pass Out' was pretty much scrapped. We went right back to the drawing board.

It was a weird time. I'd got a No. 1, but in the midst of all the success and happiness, there was also another new side to my life I had to deal with; like moving out of your house, not getting to see your family and friends so much. Everything changed...

Making The Album

Every song has an insight into Patrick – my dad forgot my birthday when I was seven, my uncle would come round and drink Kestral, my mum is 44 with no wrinkles! It's weird with music, being in the studio can bring out so many emotions. It was an opportunity, after the success of 'Pass Out', to have a moment of clarity and express that through music; to look back over all of those things that happened as a kid that stick in your memory. I wanted people to get a sense of who I am, where I've come from, what I'm about. On *Disc-Overy* you learn something about me on every single track, even if it's just one line, you learn about me or my family.

The album took six or seven months to record and I recorded it all over the place. I was recording in studios, on the tour bus, in hotel rooms after wild nights with girls... Wherever I was, I'd set up a mic, my Mac and a mixer and record the day's events. It was definitely a memorable experience.

I still listen to *Disc-Overy*. It takes me back to the calm before the storm. It's all about discovering the music industry, and my life in general. I was recording that stuff with all the hopes in the world but there was no guarantee that anything would happen. Then I watched things go colossal – 2010 was the most exciting year of my life. I had two No.1 singles, a No.1 album, I was finally getting my time at the MOBOs... As the year continued it kept getting bigger. I could go to a house music festival and play to that crowd. I was going to St. Tropez and Cannes, I was getting messages from Lindsay Lohan on Twitter. You should see the things she DMs me! I could show you DMs from sports personalities, from the cricketer Kevin Pietersen, from football players, from royalty! All the things a couple of good songs and an album can do. It's insane! Essentially though, I made a body of work that I'm really proud of and will be proud of forever.

Track By Track

Intro

In this day and age, because of the iTunes generation, albums are like 'Greatest Hits', because you'll have a Rihanna or a Gaga who have six, seven, eight singles from one album. I felt like my album definitely had those qualities, in the sense that there were loads of hits on it. But at the very beginning of the album, I wanted people to get a sense of who I was and where I'd come from. The 'Intro' was my only opportunity to do that.

We recorded it in Greenwich at our old little studio. I went in with the producer Jon (from All About She) and said a few words that were very real and honest. The lyrics are things I really wanted to say and get out of the way, before people started enjoying 'Pass Out' and 'Miami 2 Ibiza'. I put my heart and soul into it.

I think the line that strikes me most is, 'And every other day, Mummy calls me just to ask me if I'm coping with the fame...' Because she was pretty much the only one to call.

Do you know what's weird about becoming famous? People stop phoning you! It's not the other way round. They'll come to a show, but they'll never ask me for tickets – they'll always ask Dumi instead. When I see them, I'm like, 'Yo, why don't you holla at me no more?' And they just shrug. 'Well, I just thought, you're doing your thing now, and you're all around the world. I didn't think you'd want to hang out...' It staggers me. I'm still me and I still like doing the things I always did. But if there has been a change in me as a person I think it's only for the better. I'm wiser beyond my years. I'm more business-savvy, more focused, (a little bit) more organised. With a lot of artists and creative people, you'll find a lot of us are a bit head-in-the-clouds, away with the fairies! Some people might not like to admit it, but we just are. Luckily for me, I've been managed well enough by Dumi to make me stop and think a lot more.

SIMPLY UNSTOPPABLE

SIMPLE HONEY I'M A FINE BOY NO PIMPLES / I'VE DONE DEJA-VU I DONE DINGWALLS AND EVERYBODY WANTS ME ON THEIR SINGLE / MY MUM 44 YEARS WITH NO WRINKLES / I GOT A HUNDRED THOUSAND ON ME I COULD SPRINKLE ALL YEAR MY HOUSE COVERED IN TINSEL / I GONE AND POP AND I WON'T STOP PRINGLES / SO INVOLVED IN THIS MOMENT / I CANT LET IT GO / UH TICK TOCK CHECK MY ROLEY WRIST WATCH / HOW MUCH A DRINK COSTS WE ABOUT TO KICK OFF LIKE / ITS OUTRAGEOUS AND SOPHISTICATED / ITS ALL IN THE AIR / THE BIG BOSS MAKE EM JUMP LIKE KRISS KROSS / GIRL YOU BETTER TURN ME ON COS I'M ABOUT TO SWITCH OFF / I CAN'T EXPLAIN IT / SO CRAZY / (COOL) / BUT YOU'RE GONNA LOVE THIS (YES) / SO CRAZY / OUTRAGEOUS (BIG) / SIMPLY UNSTOPPABLE X2 / I THINK I SHOULD REMIND EM / I'M ABOUT TO CLEAN UP LIKE A DYSON / COS I JUST SAY HOW IT IS LIKE SIMON / I LIKE THE TASTE OF ALCOHOL / I GOT WINE GUMS / I DON'T EVA WANNA HEAR ANOTHER SIREN / THEM HIGH RISES CAN BLOCK YOUR HORIZON / DISTURBING LONDON IS THE CITY WHERE I'M FROM WHERE IF WE LIKE THE TUNE WE MAKE THE DJ REWIND EM / SO INVOLVED IN THIS MOMENT / I CANT LET IT GO / UH TICK TOCK CHECK MY ROLEY WRIST WATCH / HOW MUCH A DRINK COSTS WE ABOUT TO KICK OFF LIKE / ITS OUTRAGEOUS AND SOPHISTICATED / ITS ALL IN THE AIR / THE BIG BOSS MAKE EM JUMP LIKE KRISS KROSS / GIRL YOU BETTER TURN ME ON COS I'M ABOUT TO SWITCH OFF / I CAN'T EXPLAIN IT (COOL) / BUT YOU'RE GONNA LOVE THIS (YES) / SO CRAZY / OUTRAGEOUS (BIG) / SIMPLY UNSTOPPABLE X2 / BET I MAKE EM SAY OOOOHH / SOME ALIAS AND SOME GREY GOOSE / I SAID NO TO LIKE 6 OR 7 LABELS / I USED TO SIT NEXT TO RACHEL IN ST PAUL'S / MY FANS ARE CRAZY WITH STENCILS AND STAPLES / I CAME TO CAUSE A BIT OF CHAOS AND TO BREAK RULES / IF IT AIN'T ME IT AIN'T COOL / OI BABY, BRING ANOTHER BOTTLE TO THE TABLE

Simply Unstoppable

This track really stood out from the rest. I worked with Al Shux, who produced 'Empire State of Mind' for Jay-Z. We met at the Brits and when he asked if I wanted to work with him, there was only one answer: 'Er, yes please!'

We recorded it at his studio in Kensal Rise, north-west London. I wanted to talk about having something so good that you can't even explain it. But it was the work that Al did on this that I love most. I like things that sound weird and completely different. If I hear something that sounds slightly twisted with a little pop edge, I'm all about it. Usually within the first five seconds of hearing a song, if I can think of even one line, then it's a goer.

A lot of things I say on 'Simply Unstoppable' are both literal and metaphorical. There are a lot of double meanings like, 'got a hundred thousand on me I can sprinkle', refers to both money and cake decorations. Ambition. A lot of it is about living on a council estate. I've always been scared of estates even though I lived on one because I think the people who designed them were cruel. There's nothing good that can come out of living somewhere so grey, dingy and depressing.

Where I grew up you had a chemist, a corner shop, a doctor's surgery... you've got everything you need so you don't need to leave. The walkways are really thin and narrow, the lifts are tiny. It's built for conflict. It's almost like a camp or a prison.

I think there are some kids out there who don't know what's going on in the rest of the world. Every time I go to a school or a youth club and people ask for advice I just say, 'The world is a big place, try and see all of it.' If I had never moved to Plumstead, chances are I would have still been an MC, that I wouldn't have had the foresight that I had, that I could make music for everyone, Americans, Europeans, Australians, people all over the world.

Pass Out

'Pass Out' was never meant to be a single; everyone thought it was too hard, too 'urban'. It was like, put out the tune, give it to the specialist DJs, hopefully get it on MTV Base, do some specialist press, just to let people know Tinie's been signed and then we'll do a 'proper' first single. But, I have to say, out of the whole album, out of every song I've ever done in my whole life, 'Pass Out' is my baby. That's my first No.1 right there!

I don't know what other artists' motives are: financial, chart success, girls... but if you're not making tunes that you're not proud of, then why do it? That's what 'Pass Out' was about. I'd signed the deal, I was relaxed, in my zone. All the anxieties of being the last artist signed had gone out the window and I was signed to a label that I was a big fan of. I had this confidence and was determined to go into the studio with Lab and just do what we wanted to do. Everybody sent us in there with an idea of what they wanted, but we said 'Forget that', and did it our way.

My favourite line is: 'I'm about to be a bigger star than my mum thought... ' Because no one – not one person – predicted all of this! That's why it's so great. My most famous line is probably about the fact I've never been to Scunthorpe – I still haven't, but I will go one day! Those lines are just things that came into my head. The song is full of very real facts about me. I don't know where they came from!

I think I might have mentioned this track once or twice throughout this book. Ha! So, you know a lot about it already. But that just goes to show how important it is to me, in so many different ways. This was the song that changed everything. It took me places.

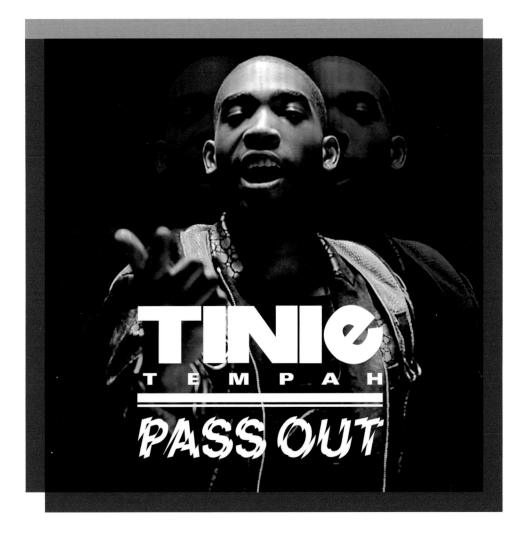

Illusion

This was another track I worked on with Al Shux, but we also got someone else very special on board – Luke Steele from Empire of the Sun. I met Luke at Oxegen Festival and I loved his attitude. I was like, 'I'm a big fan. If I send you a track can you just do something on it?' Luke was so cool. He said, 'Of course, you don't even have to credit me, I just want to do it.'

We also worked with an English songwriter called Sam Frank – it was quite a weird combination. Like a big mix of hip-hop, indie, drums and piano. It was a real mish-mash, but the results were incredible.

Lyrically, I nodded my head hard at the Canadian artist Drake. In 2009, he released a mixtape called 'So Far Gone' and it was revolutionary. Here was a hip-hop artist not talking about guns and shootings, knives and killing. He was talking about life in such detail and so visually. It was the most honest piece of work I'd heard from a new rapper, apart from Kanye West of course. I used to bang out that mixtape in my little Vauxhall Corsa. I'd always been about being true to who I was and Drake reiterated to me that you can be yourself and still be a superstar.

The dark side of life always appears to be glamorous when you're young. Especially when you're in school and you see girls that you fancy in class waiting outside for guys with mopeds who ain't in school for some reason. In secondary school, there are new networks that spring up. You meet people who are not always the most positive people. Me and my friends did a few silly things, just a few fights or hanging around the streets, but after a while I was like, *I just want to be a musician.* Hanging around on street corners with 10 other guys and no girls ain't fun – it's cold! And that's what I'm talking about when I say, 'With dishonest youths, doing things I didn't want to do/Wishing I could see the world from a different point of view...'

Just A Little

This track is about a girl that I was seeing just before 'Pass Out' was released. I had a lot more time on my hands back then, so I was around her house a lot, and she'd come to my house to cook for me. She'd even make food for my dad! She's the best girl in the world. The perfect girl, really. She was a singer as well, and was releasing a song around about the same time as 'Pass Out'. Her brothers would tease us, saying, 'Oh yeah, we'll see what happens when you both release your song in the charts, who does better.' Before 'Pass Out' came out, I realised it was better to stop seeing her before things got complicated. 'You know what, babe,' I said. 'Let's still be friends but let's not take this any further.'

I love girls, I love them, but it's just not possible for me to have a girlfriend at the moment. One day, I'll be married with kids, but while my life is so hectic and I'm all over the world, it's not fair to anyone for me to be with someone. Until I can treat a girl respectfully and be fully involved, I can't have a girlfriend. And that's what I tried to explain in this song.

We went to Sweden to record this and me and Dumi had to share a really, really tiny hotel room with two single beds for five days. We were ready to just kill each other by the end! But it was fun and I got to see another part of Europe – I saw snow six foot deep. We had the biggest snowball fight ever. I'd never seen anything like it. It was insane.

"Girl, I don't wanna be no hero."

Snap

We made 'Snap' in Greenwich, London. Photos paint a thousand words. You look at a photo and what you see and what I see are going to be two completely different things, but it's still just the one photo.

Over the last year or two, photos have been the most important thing to me. It's been the best way for me to capture the moment. Everything happens so fast, so if you don't take a picture, it's gone forever. You can do a video, but videos give too much away whereas a photo is subjective. What was he thinking? What was going on in his mind? So 'Snap' stresses the importance of that and what photos mean to me. It was my opportunity to really go into about where I came from as well, and my mum and my dad. It's almost an ode to my father and a little acknowledgement that he done his bit, he had his shop and that inspired me as a person: he got his grey hair doing something he believed in. The part about my mum and dad's wedding photo being so lovely balances out the parts about the troubles they had. The wedding photo is so beautiful; it's my favourite photo in the world.

"*These moments and memories we keep.*"

Written In The Stars

In this song, I wanted people to know that I was a young guy trying to live out his dream and do everything possible to make that dream happen. I'm from London, one of the most amazing cities in the world, and it's given me all these opportunities. It's one of the only places in the world where you can live in a council block and see a beautiful Victorian house across the street. Growing up around that was inspirational, it kept me motivated. I'm trying to live the dream and other people can do the same if they put their mind to it. I'm a pretty average guy, I like everything to be easy, but at the same time I want it all and I'm going to do everything in my power to make sure that that happens.

The producer on the song, iSHi, teamed me up with Eric Turner and we just clicked straight away. Our relationship is very cool. I really love what he did on the track and I felt like what he did was so powerful that it really made sense having him on the road. When we went to No.1, it was a weird week. iSHi was in London and we went to the Sanderson Hotel with Dumi and Eric. 'Do you remember when we had the party for "Pass Out" and I told you we'd get our No.1? Well, I think we're about to,' I said to iSHi. That song sold more in the first week than 'Pass Out'. I think it did 100,000 copies in the first week. Insane!

One of the standout lyrics for me is: 'When they see me everybody brap braps/ Man I'm like a young and fully black Barack.' Everyone knows what that means, right? Okay, for those that don't, I'll explain it in my very best English: 'Brap brap' is like a colloquial term of excitement and exaltation; when you really like something and you get really excited about something, chances are you go 'brap brap'.

Making the video for 'Written In The Stars' in New York.

The producer on the song, iSHi, teamed me up with Eric Turner and we just clicked straight away. Our relationship is very cool. I really love what he did on the track and I felt like what he did was so powerful.

Frisky

'Frisky' is more or less about doing a show and going to an after party and just having fun, good old laddish fun. I was annoyed that 'Frisky' lost out to Dizzee and James Cordon's World Cup Song, 'Shout' in getting to No.1, but I also wasn't. As an artist, you have to have somewhere to look forward to. I think I need to have that 'Arrrrghhhh, just missed it!' feeling to make me work harder. Plus, it's not that bad when you come second to Dizzee Rascal. I've got to be happy with that. It got a lot of praise too; Chris Martin from Coldplay said, 'Great gym track, great gym album.' Some people said that it sounded too much like 'Pass Out', but what sounds like 'Pass Out'? Nothing! Exactly.

This song has one of my most famous lines in it: 'Would you risk it for a chocolate biscuit?' No one really knows what that line means. I know why I said it, but I've never told anyone. It's just a personal joke and it became the biggest part of the song. Obviously it's a very British thing – only we would talk about biscuits. But the initial reason why I said it, I've never told anybody that and I never will. Sorry guys!

"Would you risk it for a chocolate biscuit?"

Miami 2 Ibiza

Swedish House Mafia basically are the rock stars of the dance world and working on this tune with them was out of this world. They have this mad energy that I've never seen in my life. Watching them in action is genius. The three of them sit next to each other in a line with their headphones on and their MacBook Pros, and then once in a while, one of them will scream something in Swedish and then play this amazing bass line and they all scream. Then they all work around that. It's like watching a factory produce music. After we made it, they decided they wanted it for their second single. Their energy was crazy; they got me in the zone.

I had the opportunity to roll with them on a few shows and it's all private jet this, Rolex that, Ferraris, Louis Vuitton... They are on a whole other spectrum. It's a bit racy in parts this song; I talk about a girl wanting to see what's hiding in my CK briefs... but you've got to be a bit cheeky now and then.

"I got a black BM, she got a white TT."

Obsession

If I had to pick one song I wasn't so keen on any more, it would be 'Obsession'. It was written at a dark time for me. Emile Hayne produced and he does a lot of KiD CuDi's stuff. Emile's a very cool guy and we made it in Soho Studios in London. We were in there for just one night and 'Obsession' was the end result of that. But I do think the song is very dark, maybe too dark, and I said things that maybe I should have kept inside. That said, it absolutely reflects what I was thinking at that time, and that was something I really wanted *Disc-Overy* to do, so no regrets.

I think I might have been a bit too vocal, like when I say, 'My daddy was present but sometimes forget me presents, like when I was seven... ' It's the worst to be forgotten as a kid. I held that with me. For my seventh birthday, I got no presents, nothing. I don't know how my dad feels about it, though, I've never mentioned it to him. If he's heard that line on the record he's never said anything. I was a total mummy's boy when I was younger and when I didn't get presents that day I became bitter towards my dad. Maybe it was a hard year financially. I suppose I never stopped to consider that.

The track says a lot about my personality, too. When I say, 'Cos nine out of ten times I don't even get me', I'm talking about how erratic I can be. If I wasn't so well managed I'd be off somewhere, who knows where. The number of times things have gone crazy in America and I've gone to the wrong gate at the airport and nearly ended up in Alaska. But then my mind wonders... 'Hmm'. Sometimes the idea of buying a ticket and disappearing somewhere can be quite appealing.

Invincible

We recorded this one at our Disturbing London studios with iSHi. There was no real plan, but it ended up being beautiful. I think 'Invincible' was more for the people who liked me off the back of 'Wifey'. What's amazing about 'Invincible' is that when you release songs like 'Pass Out' and 'Miami 2 Ibiza', tracks like 'Invincible' fall down the list of songs you really want to perform. But when you do get to do a big set, it's nice to slow down and see people get their lighters out and wave.

'Invincible' is basically a song for all of my fans and it's basically me just saying to you guys, 'Together we stand, divided we fall.' Without you guys I wouldn't be here and I thank you for being that support structure I needed from the very beginning. You've carried me all the way to where I am now. One thing people don't understand is that in certain places in the world 'Invincible' is bigger than 'Pass Out', it's so weird. What I've seen around the world is that you need to make loads of different music in loads of different styles. Only in England is 'Pass Out' the biggest song.

I'm so glad this gave me the opportunity to work with Kelly Rowland too. I just hope she doesn't go all superstar on me because of *X Factor*!

"I feel like the brightest star."

Wonderman

This was another effort from me and Lab, but this time Ellie Goulding came on board. I got her down to the studio and it all went a bit weird. She started singing her bit and the next thing I know her legs are up in the air and then Labrinth's legs were up in the air. I was like, 'What the hell is going on?' I have no idea what they were doing. It looked like they'd stopped to do some kind of aerobic class or something. I ended up walking out, saying 'Guys, I'm going to go, just send it to me when it's done!' I had to leave those two weirdos to it!

'Wonderman' itself is basically about the struggle. It was made the day after 'Pass Out' went to No.1, so you can really hear that hunger. One thing that's amazing about the album is that you can hear the tracks made before and after 'Pass Out'; in some places you can hear the ambition and in others the confidence. I think there's a lot of insecurity on 'Wonderman', that's one thing I wanted people to get from the album. I was 21, so there was still lots that I was learning. It's the struggle, how hard it had to be, how hard I had to work to get where I am, and what I plan to do whilst I'm here.

It sounds weird, but I was trying to resist this fame thing for so long. I wanted success but I didn't want my life to change significantly. 'I'm walking down Bethnal Green Road,' I'd say to Dumi when he rung to see where I was. 'T! Come on, what are you doing? You can't do that.' So I can't walk about so much, I can't go to certain nightclubs and I can't just pick up a microphone if I want to do a random PA. So there's been a lot of accepting fate and 'Wonderman' is definitely about that.

Let Go

'Let Go' is another special track that's very close to my heart. It's a very important song to me and it was the perfect track to close the album with. Emeli Sandé, who did vocals on there, is sick. I think she's one of the best talents in the country, by far.

It's a personal letter to my fans. When you become successful, you become the property of the public to an extent. I don't always want to stick around after gigs because I want to get on with making it perfect. There's also a bit of insecurity in there too: the sacrifices you have to make, like not seeing your family, the way that girls start acting, and how everybody wants to know you because you're 'famous'.

'Why do I feel more safe on stage than in my own living room...' captures a lot really. I feel invincible every time I go out on stage. I feel like no one can do anything to me. I've got 10,000 of the very best friends you could have. By contrast, when I'm at home, well, fame can be a crazy thing. Before anything big, I can't sleep, I get anxious, I can't breathe properly sometimes. It's when you're on your own that anxieties creep in.

But, as always, family are never far away from my thoughts and in this song I reveal a little bit about my granny. 'My grandma say if I leave my drink I shouldn't sip again...'

My granny, rest her soul, always used to say that. It's a Nigerian superstition. If you have a drink and you put it down to go to the toilet or go somewhere and come back, you shouldn't sip it again. So I never do. Ever!

There's some stuff about my brother in there, too. 'I even notice physical differences in my siblings/ That's why I feel so down even at the top of the Rivington...'

My brother's like six foot tall now. I've literally missed a big part of him growing up. As a big brother, I wish I was there for him more, answering questions about girls and life. I really miss my family. But then 'If music needed saving I'd die for it...' I've given up so much for music, I honestly do think I could die for it.

Making The Videos

When you first shoot a video, it's the most exciting thing in the world. I love doing it and I really love seeing the end result, but it can also be a very long day. Also, imagine you shoot a video to release in the summer, chances are you would have to film it during the winter. So you can get a bit confused! But while it's long days, you get to meet cool make-up artists and directors, stylists and actors or extras. You get to see the directors at work and watch the footage back and sometimes if you're working with a good director he could even be editing as you go along – that's fun. I get really involved in the concept of a video. Initially, I talk to Dumi about what I see happening, he talks about what he sees for it, and we eventually agree on something. Then we present that to the video commissioner, and he talks to a director. Next, we'll get lots of proposals come through from how the professionals see it working. Some ideas will be bang on, some will be not so great, just very clichéd or things you've seen time and time again. We just pick the best one of the bunch.

Pass Out

This is my favourite video so far. It was so cheap really. We had £9,000 and made it with so little fuss. It became a cult thing. I remember the happiest feeling when I saw it on Q's TV station because they only play rock bands! I just had loads of MCs there and it was a very gritty video in the end. Wretch came down, Skepta came down, JME, Sincere, Labrinth, of course... they were all supportive and egging me on, wanting me to do well and it went on to do everything for me.

It was a really cold day and I had to take my top off, so I was freezing for most of the morning. Tim Brown directed it, and there were lots of graphic elements mixed in with live action. It started out getting a few thousand views, and then suddenly, it was 100,000, 200,000, a million. As we all know, it became my official first single. It's now had over 30 million views!

Written In The Stars

The video is really epic: the story is about fulfilling your dreams against all odds. A lot of people might say you can't do this or that, but if you focus and keep a tunnel vision, you can fulfil your dreams. I chose to shoot it in New York to show that it can happen anywhere in the world.

It's about a young kid called Sir who is the product of success. It's a bit like what Jay-Z said about New York, how if you can make it there, you can pretty much make it anywhere. When we filmed it, it was summer but the single was coming out in winter, so I'm wearing a leather jacket on a rooftop in New York when it was 100 degrees! I don't think I've ever sweated so much in my whole life!

2:39 / 3:37   360p

Miami 2 Ibiza

This was in theory the most fun video I've made. If you watch it, you'll see girls, speedboats, people diving into water, clubs, champagne... It's so glamorous, but guess where I filmed it? In Sweden against a boring white backdrop! I don't know why I had to go to Sweden to do that. They could have left me in London, surely! But they flew me to Sweden and I'm thinking, *Okay, I'm going to be in a club with the Swedish House Mafia and loads of girls,* but during the course of the flight, which is two hours, things changed and when I landed I was told all the cool bits would all be filmed later on in Miami and Ibiza. So that was that! This job I have can be very weird sometimes!

Wonderman

It was inspired by **The Six Million Dollar Man** because 'Wonderman' is my superhero moment on the album. It's my Clark Kent moment, accepting my fate for what it is. Even if this all ends tomorrow, it was my fate to have made music and to have become famous. But I also want to be normal and have a normal life and a normal girlfriend, only this big world's like 'No!'

The director came up with the idea of being somebody normal and dying and then being rebuilt from the ground up. That's kind of what happens when you become an artist – you're in a weird way, born again. The phoenix turns to ashes and you become a new person and so the concept off the back of this was 'Wonderman'. It isn't set in a specific time or place. It's a timeless video. More importantly, being the last video I did for the album it had to be creative enough to be able to go anywhere from there. If I wanna be naked for my first video off the second album then... well, maybe it wouldn't be that much of a bad idea! If I want to do that I could, because 'Wonderman' left me in such a weird creative place.

Recognition

If you haven't gathered already, a lot of hard work from a lot of people went into my debut album. So it was the best day of my life when I found out the album had gone to No.1. It sold 85,000 copies in the first week! Rappers in America aren't even selling 85,000 in the first week! Everyone from the label was so excited, they were going to present me with a gold plaque but because it went platinum so quickly, we skipped the gold disc and went straight to platinum. This is at a time when it's really not easy to sell albums.

I think there's a number of things that made it happen like that – the right singles at the right times. 'Pass Out' became like the nation's anthem for that year. It was used for Formula 1, for the Olympics, football programmes, TV series... for everything. 'Miami 2 Ibiza' opened me up to the ravers, while 'Written In The Stars' showed off my more epic, pop side. 'Pass Out' was released in March, and *Disc-Overy* didn't come out until October, so people got to know me and see my personality during those months. When it went to No.1, we went raving to celebrate – but we didn't go too nuts. It was a quiet one, just me, Dumi, Isaac and a few of my boys.

Plus there were all the awards too! I feel like my album has ticked all the boxes now. *Disc-Overy* has done everything a debut album could have done: it's gone double platinum, it's been nominated for every award, from the BRITS to the Mercury, Ivor Novello, MOBOs... everything.

I am critical, though. Looking back, I think for a first offering it was great. If I could go back and change a few lyrics and stuff, I probably would. I definitely feel that the second album is going to be better lyrically and musically. The doors to collaborate are open to me, and also as you get older, you get more experienced, musically – so hopefully we should be in for a lot more with the next album. I can't wait for you guys to hear it!

Team Effort

There have been other songs that I've done beyond my album, by teaming up with other artists and bands. Each experience has been wildly different, but so much fun too. You learn so much from other people...

Gorillaz: 'Clint Eastwood'

Damon Albarn has always been pretty interested in me and my music; he always wants to be kept in the loop with everything I'm doing. 'I don't think you should do that, this is where I think this person went wrong,' he'll tell me. Damon is always giving me advice about music and who I should and shouldn't collaborate with.

I've always respected him cos he's a rock star. A proper, certified rock star! At the GQ Men Of The Year Awards, Gorillaz won an award and so everyone was trying to go up and talk to him, all these industry people, fashion types and of course loads and loads of girls cos they all fancy him! 'Just wait, I'm talking to Tinie,' he said to every single person that came up. 'So anyway, Tinie, where were we... ' We were talking for about 25 minutes! So he's always been a really cool, down to earth dude.

He called me one day, 'We're gonna do "Clint Eastwood" on Jonathan Ross and we want you to do the rap.' It was amazing but I remember being under so much pressure to make sure I wrote something of Gorillaz's standard – they do some of the best collaborations in the world. So I did it, I recorded it on my Mac, then I went into a studio and vocalled it. 'Yes, good boy, this is wicked,' Damon grinned.

When we went to do Jonathan Ross, I was in the green room with Jamie Hewlett, who does all of the Gorillaz's artwork. My palms were so sweaty and I think I must have gone to the toilet five times! With TV, they usually give you a couple of tries to get it right, but we nailed it the first time. Damon even dropped the mic stand but it was so perfect that he was like, 'Just keep it.' Afterwards I got to meet Jonathan Ross who was wearing a tracksuit, which was pretty cool and a bit weird cos he always wears suits!

Chase & Status: 'Hitz'

I was supporting them on tour and we'd met very briefly at the first show in Camden, but for two seconds because it was right before I went on stage. The second time we met on tour it was in Bournemouth and it was really awkward, I didn't even say hello! But we met a bunch of times after that and when they asked me to be involved with their album I said yes straight away.

I remember receiving the song. They had said about all these amazing people on their album, from Cee-Lo to Dizzee. So I remember I wrote the first verse and I went to their studio – it's a proper nice studio and they gave me peppermint tea! – with the first verse to get their approval. I rapped it to them and they were like 'Yeah, yeah, this is good', so I wrote the second verse in front of them and it was just hard; flaunting a little bit.

The video was amazing to do, too! Now, what normally happens when you finish shooting is they're like 'It's a wrap' and usually there's drinks afterwards so I was like, 'Yeahhhhhh, let's party!' They were trying to pretend they'd only had two hours' sleep and were too tired. Saul actually told me he was coming out but he didn't. I wanted these guys to come out for a little bit of raving – they really missed out. We had a very good time!

JLS: 'Eyes Wide Shut'

More than anything, me and JLS get on. We're friends. Me and Marvin are from the same area in Plumstead and the other boys I've known for a few years. They're just wicked, normal boys, they are so laid back, and they haven't changed despite all the fame. And they aren't afraid to share their success either – they did four O2 Arena shows and they got me to come out for every single performance of that track. They go three-times-platinum every time they release an album and it was a really nice thing for me to do, a really great opportunity.

Chapter Five:

LIFE ON THE ROAD

WHEN ALL
YOU GUYS SING
EVERY WORD BACK,
IT'S INCREDIBLE.
THE FIRST TIME IT
HAPPENED I HAD
GOOSE BUMPS
OVER MY
WHOLE BODY.

Once my album was finally out there, I took the songs to my fans on my very own headline tour. The Disc-Overy tour took me all around the country – Cardiff, Newcastle, Edinburgh, Manchester, Birmingham, Lincoln, Liverpool... but still not Scunthorpe, sorry!

I'm used to playing live. As a teenager I did all those gigs all over the country, in schools and in nightclubs, for anything from 12 people to a few hundred. Then, it went to the thousands when I supported Chipmunk, Chase & Status, Usher and Rihanna. In the middle of all that, I started playing my own headline shows, not just in Britain, but all over Europe and at festivals for fans of all types of music.

Playing live is absolutely the best part of making music. Seeing all those people enjoying something you've created. It's the most amazing sight ever. But of course it's not just about being on stage, lots of stuff happens when you're on the road...

The Crew

I've got a really close team that always come on the road with me. We're a proper little unit. A lot of them are people I've been friends with for years. And what's nice is that we're all young, so none of us are jaded, none of us feel like we've been there, done that. Dumi is always there, of course. When aren't we together? He just does what he always does – looks out for me.

Charlesy is my DJ, he's also my right-hand man, my partner in crime. He's a lot of fun to be around, a real light-hearted guy who loves a laugh. He's the life and soul of the party and likes to make sure everybody else has fun. If someone has an empty glass, he'll be the one to fill it. He's just that kind of guy. I met him while I was supporting N-Dubz. He was doing a DJ set between slots and I could see he was very talented, very technical. He also knows how to fix anything – phones, cameras, ANYTHING. He's reluctant to change but he's always changing. Not so long ago, he was like 'You're wearing Chinos? I would never wear Chinos...' Two weeks later he's got Chinos on! He's a great guy.

Isaac is my road manager. He makes sure I'm always all right, that I've got everything I need. He's a really nice guy, like a big teddy bear. He used to live on Dumi's mum's road and when things started going well for us, he went to Dumi's mum's house and told Obi (Dumi's younger brother) that he wanted to help out. He started out driving us around, picking things up and before you knew it, he became part of the team.

Josh is my musical director and drummer – he's also Labrinth's brother. We like to keep things in the family! He likes to drum standing up with a backpack on, which is unusual, but whatever works for him. He's very loud and outgoing and always likes to be the centre of attention. He's the first person you notice when you're in a room with him. He's a very honest guy too, wears his heart on his sleeve. If he feels there's something wrong he'll have to say. He's the first to stand up if he feels something isn't fair.

These guys do so much more for me than just be part of my band or manage me – they're my brothers. Life on the road wouldn't be half as much fun without them!

Charlesy, Isaac, Dumi, Josh, Obi & my band: life on the road wouldn't be half as much fun without them!

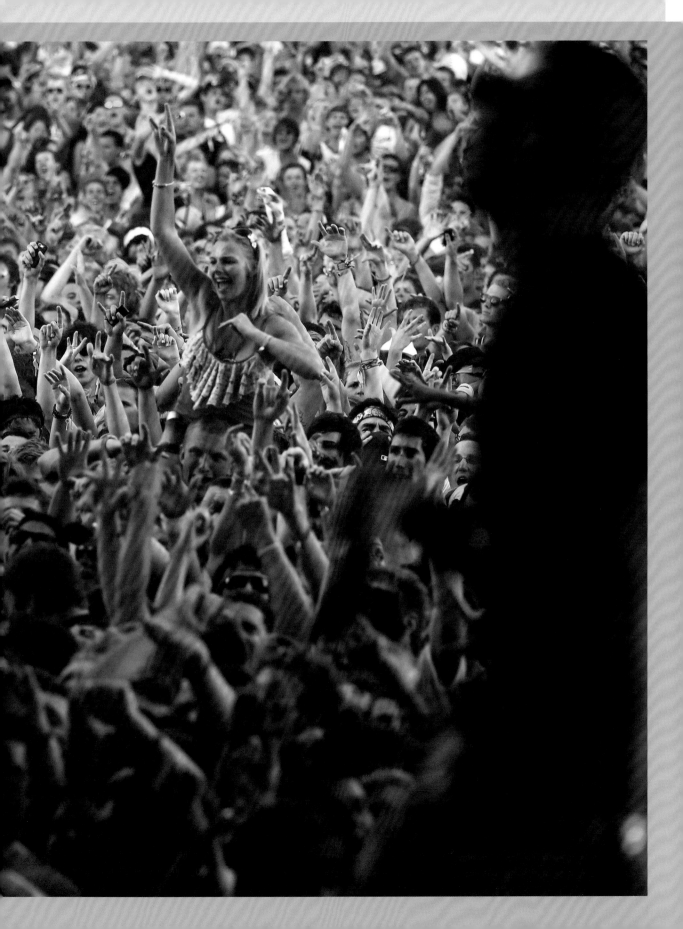

The Tour Bus

More recently, we've been lucky enough to occasionally get around by more luxurious forms of transport, like private jets! But the tour bus really is the best thing in the world. It's where all the biggest laughs happen. We have so many dumb stories from our travels.

The first tour bus we had was so rubbish. We were on tour for ages and when it came to taking our bags out of the loading boots for the last time, there was this really strange smell in the air. We realised that everyone's bags smelled like wee! It turns out someone had done a poo in the toilet and it had blocked it and a pipe had burst. You're only supposed to do number ones in tour bus toilets, never a number two! Thank God, I didn't put my bag there!

The driver was this guy called Jim who was the dirtiest guy I've ever seen – literally. He was like a kid who had been playing outside in the mud. We pulled the bedsheets off the bus and washed them at a dry-cleaner's. We had clean, fresh sheets and it's those kind of things that make living in a cramped space just that little bit easier. I recommend that to anyone on a tour bus!

Now I've moved up a bit. I get my own room in the back, a double bed and a TV – oh yeah! It's fun. We don't play much music because there's too many of us and it causes arguments. Plus we all have headphones and laptops, so if you want to listen to music, you just do that. We play computer games, a lot of NBA and Street Fighter. There's a hard-drive full of films so we're always arguing about what films we're going to watch. I'm into my rom-coms. The last one I watched was *Date Night* with Steve Carell. Is it weird that I like rom-coms so much? It probably is, but there's nothing I can do about it. I love them!

My Rider

So when you get to the venue you're playing at, in the dressing room there's usually some goodies waiting for you – your rider! You get to request these things, too. This is what I always ask for:

- **Butterkist popcorn:** *sweet not salty. I love it.*
- **Baby wipes:** *you just can never get enough baby wipes. Use them on your trainers, armpits… they're all-purpose!*
- **Eucalyptus and cotton wool:** *I put it up my nose and breathe. It just clears everything out.*
- **Lemon, honey and ginger:** *for my voice.*
- **Tea:** *because you know I love it!*
- **Sandwiches:** *I have coronation chicken on my rider but I've never gotten coronation chicken. I always get chicken caesar! It's been a year and I still never get coronation chicken – even on my own tours! I should have a fit, shouldn't I?*
- **Rowntree's Randoms:** *they're my favourite sweets.*
- **Nando's:** *obviously.*
- **A basketball net:** *now I'm doing arena tours, I'm going to ask for one because those venues are so big. While you're waiting you could be having a little game with the boys and crew.*

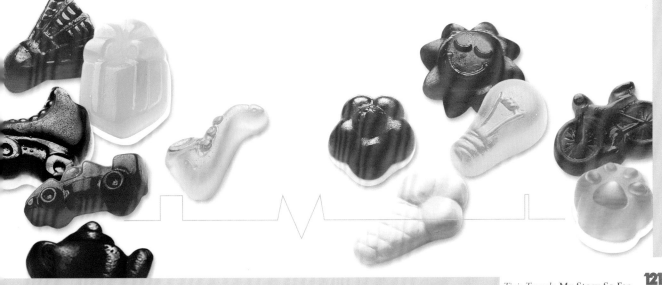

Warm-Up

Before I go on stage, I get everyone into one room. We all have a little drink and a toast together. The bigger the event, the more special that toast is. Sometimes, we have a little prayer or a Jack Daniels! I like telling random jokes or secrets, something to get rid of the insecurities. 'Tell me something I don't know about you...' those kinds of games. It gets everyone laughing and loosened up.

The arena shows are going to be special. When we do the London O2 Arena, I want everyone there: Dizzee, Chipmunk, Ironik, Wretch, Professor Green, Skepta... every MC has to be there. They have so many dressing rooms in those places, everyone can have their own dressing room and we can all hang out together and have a laugh. When I do the O2, that's going to be a big day for everyone.

Once we've all gotten together, because the band have to go on stage before me, I get 15 minutes to myself to work on my vocals. Because my cousin Henry goes to RADA, he's taught me lots of vocal exercises to loosen up my mouth and tongue. He's probably talking rubbish but I do them anyway!

I like telling random jokes or
secrets, something to get rid of
the insecurities. 'Tell me something
don't know about you...' those kinds
of games. It gets everyone laughing
and loosened up.

Showtime

Just before I go on, I always do an extra sign of the cross when I'm by the side of the stage. Whether we've done a prayer or not, when I hear 'Tinie! Tinie! Tinie!' I always cross myself.

Sean Ryder was on before me at V Festival and he got booed off halfway through his set. 'I dunno what you've done to them, but they love you, good luck!' he said, as he came off stage. I was like, *I can't believe this is happening, all these people wanna see me!* It's an incredible feeling.

I don't get as nervous any more, unless it's a really big show, but I always get butterflies. When I perform 'Written In The Stars', there's a bit where Charlesy cuts the music and I hold the microphone out to the crowd. When all you guys sing every word back, it's incredible. The first time it happened I had goose bumps over my whole body. It makes you feel incredibly emotional. My favourite song to perform is 'Frisky'. There are so many things in the song for the crowd to do – lots of audience interaction.

If I think back to me, aged 14, writing my first lyric – which was rubbish! – to almost a decade later and I'm playing all over the world for people that have bought all of my records, watched all of my videos and know every word... it's humbling. It's exciting and it's beyond my wildest, wildest expectations. I absolutely love performing and being on stage. It's the best part of the job, no doubt at all.

Come Down

The minute I get off stage, I don't wanna talk to journalists or hang out with label people, I just want to see my friends and the band. But, usually, there are some fans waiting at the stage door for autographs and photos, which I'm always up for. It's nice for me to have the chance to say thanks, too.

The weirdest place I've been asked to sign is probably, well, girls' boobs. It's a bit embarrassing, but I do get asked to do that a lot from my older female fans. I do have the best fans though. I get sent a lot of presents, things that people have found out I like, like Paco Rabanne's aftershave, 1 Million. I probably have about 20 boxes of it because people found out I like it and sent it to me. I get fancy facial creams or people will read fashion blogs and know what clothes I like to wear and send T-shirts or trainers. The best present though is from a girl called Lucy. She made me this incredible scrapbook, which covers everything from my first-ever show to my first-ever headline tour. It's awesome.

After meeting the fans, when we're on tour, we usually get straight onto the tour bus. Because everything is so new, we're all as excited as each other. In the early days, we would do a lot of partying and go clubbing as well. Most times now, we'll have a little party on the tour bus as we drive through the night to the next venue. It's great. You go to sleep in one city and wake up somewhere else entirely.

Chapter Six:

WHO I AM

This book is all me, the total 100 per cent truth.

40% Family

40% Family and friends. They are absolutely the most important part of my life; without them, everything else would mean absolutely nothing.

30% Music: I really would die for music. It's such a huge, massive part of my life.

15% Fashion: I love clothes, trainers, watches, sunglasses... I really love getting dressed up for a fancy night out. But I also love a nice pair of Nikes, shorts and a T-shirt. Nice and simple.

10% Partying and food: Well, you can't live without either, right?

5% Girls: Women, women, women. I really love women. Gosh, girls, you are actually amazing!

30% Music

15% Fashion

10% Partying

5% Girls

The reason I wanted to write this book was not only to reflect on the crazy journey I've been on over the last 22 years, but to give you guys more of an insight into me and what makes me tick. This book is all me, the total 100 per cent truth. You're getting everything from Patrick to Tinie and back again. Here's a bit of what makes me tick…

Fashion

A big love of mine is clothes. I'd describe my style as a fine balance between street cool culture and high-end fashion. I like to mix and match. I'm very observant wherever I go – New York, London, Paris, Stockholm, Milan, Copenhagen – it's good to watch what people wear. I try my best to find a balance between things that are high-end like a Rolex or an authentic wax Barbour, and vintage clothing mixed with Nike Air Force 1's or Nike Blazers. It's meant to look accessible but when you decode it a bit, it's not.

At the moment, I like wearing leather jackets. The most expensive piece of clothing I own is a £2,000 leather jacket from Barneys in New York. I don't always get it right. My worst fashion faux-pas was a velour tracksuit. I did it guys, I can't lie. I did wear velour tracksuits! Thank God these days, I have a stylist to help me out.

As a musician I've always expressed myself even when it wasn't really considered a cool thing to wear fitted jeans or certain coloured tops. I used to get quite a bit of stick for it. 'Why do you wear them Ray-Bans? I'll never wear Ray-Bans bruv,' Chipmunk said to me once. I made him try a pair on, I even took a picture and told him they suited him. 'Nah bruv, I'll never wear Ray-Bans.' A year later, he's wearing Ray-Bans! Now Professor Green and Dappy are wearing them, and Ashley Cole is wearing clear specs! I just love clothes and I like that I'm not afraid to try and be different.

Jacket - Albam
T-Shirt - American Apparel
Jeans - D Squared
Belt - Folk
Trainers - Nike Blazers

THE MOST EXPENSIVE PIECE OF CLOTHING I OWN IS A £2,000 LEATHER JACKET FROM BARNEYS IN NEW YORK

Blazer - Tim Soar
T-shirt - American Apparel
Shorts - Christopher Kane
Glasses - Cutler and Gross
Trainers - Nike Blazers
Bag - Louis Vuitton

ME IN MY WORDS:

Honest, humble, down to earth, fun-loving, modest, likes to party, loves girls, kind, good listener, grateful, thankful, appreciative, funny.

Designing My Own Clothes

These days I design my own clothes! I'd wanted to create a clothing line for a long time, so as soon as we could, me and Dumi set up the Disturbing London line. We've got some really great T-shirts out there with our logo that I feel so proud to wear on stage. The whole thing is about street cool and high-end fashion mixed together. We've done things like cotton tracksuits, which look smart enough to wear out to a club. We have T-shirts, jackets and cool denim stuff. Some of the clothing has no logo on it, so it's very subtle.

Biker Jacket - Surface 2 Air
T-Shirt - Disturbing London
Jeans - D Squared
Glasses - Linda Farrow Luxe
Trainers - Air Jordan III

Designing your own clothes is actually a lot simpler than you imagine. I know what I like - the fit of a shirt, how high a zip goes - so we'll get sketches made up and try to get our hands at something similar. I basically take a bit of inspiration from other designs I like but give them my own unique twist.

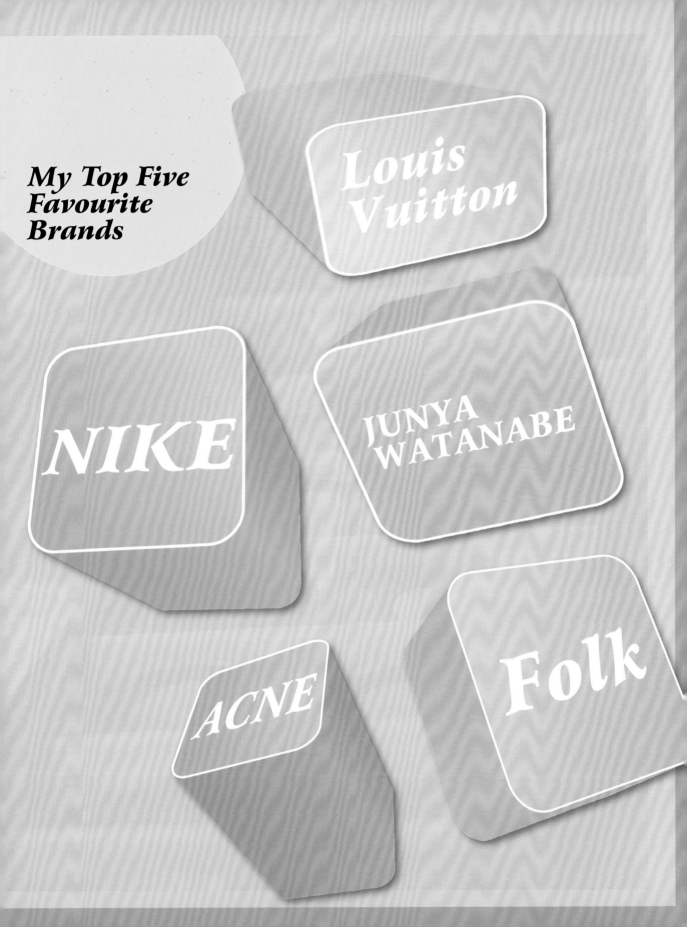

My Top Five
Favourite
Brands

Louis
Vuitton

NIKE

JUNYA
WATANABE

ACNE

Folk

★ *My top five **male** fashion icons*

Kanye

Hurts

Pharrell

Reggie

Dumi

♥ *My top five female fashion icons*

♥ *Jameela*

♥ *Shingai*

♥ *Alexa Chung*

♥ *Yasmin*

♥ *Emma Watson*

Music

I don't really need to say this, because *obviously* music is a huge passion of mine. I listen to it all day every day and it's such a mixture of stuff. I'll listen to anything and everything. You can't create new music yourself without inspiration and what amazes me is how many talented British artists there are out there at the moment. Plus, music is so powerful, your happiest and saddest memories often get attached to a song. My tastes change every day, but right now this is what I'm all about...

My Favourite Albums

Adele: **21**
Big Sean: **Finally Famous**
Rick Ross: **Teflon Don**
Kanye & Jay-Z: **Watch The Throne**
Wretch 32: **Black & White**
Katy B: **On A Mission**
Arcade Fire: **The Suburbs**
James Blake: **James Blake**
Jamie Woon: **Mirrorwriting**
Chase & Status: **No More Idols**
Amy Winehouse: **Back To Black**
Michael Bublé: **Crazy Love**
The Streets: **Original Pirate Material**
Angus & Julia Stone: **Heart Full Of Wine**
Stevie Wonder: **Songs In The Key Of Life**
Young Jeezy: **Thug Motivation 101**

My First Record

So Solid Crew:
They Don't Know

My Latest Record

Queen: **Greatest Hits**

The Song That Reminds Me Of My Mum

Dolly Parton: '9 to 5'. My mum brought me up on Dolly Parton. I love her. So when Dolly was in London, I managed to arrange for my mum to meet her. I think it made my mum very, very happy.

My Most Embarrassing Record

Justin Bieber: **My World.** I love him!

The Song That Reminds Me Of My Dad

Kool and the Gang: **'Celebration'.** That's like every older black person's favourite song!

The Song I Want Played At My Funeral

Well, I'm going to live to 102 by the grace of God! And I'll have a grieving 20-year-old widow. But when the time comes, I want Israel Kamakawiwo'ole's version of **'Somewhere Over The Rainbow'**. It's so beautiful.

The Song I Want For My First Wedding Dance

'Wifey'! As a joke, of course!

Pea Coat - Liberty of London
T-Shirt - Ksubi
Glasses - Cutler and Gross

The Songs That Reminds Me Of My Childhood

The Spice Girls! Everytime I hear **'Wannabe'**, it makes me feel young again. Michael Jackson was like the soundtrack to my youth, especially, **'Smooth Criminal'**. Salt-N-Pepa's **'Let's Talk About Sex'** takes me right back too. It reminds me of being a kid cos they used to always play that one at African parties.

The Albums That Inspired Me Most

This probably sounds cheesy but honestly it's the first album of every MC I know. Kano - **Home Sweet Home**, Dizzee - **Boy In Da Corner**, Tinchy - **Catch 22** and Chipmunk - **I Am Chipmunk**. My album came out after all these guys and I'm glad I had the opportunity to learn from, and be inspired by, them all.

The Songs I Wish I'd Written

'Black or White' by Michael Jackson, Robyn **'Don't F****** Tell Me What To Do'**, Lykke Li **'Little Bit'** and Adele's whole album, **21**.

The Song That Makes Me Cry

Fyfe Dangerfield's cover of Billy Joel's **'She's Always A Woman'**. The one from the John Lewis advert, it's so beautiful!

Artists I'd Like To Collaborate With

Kanye West, **Adele**, **Jay-Z**, **Lil Wayne**, **Drake**. I'd also like to work with a singer with a beautiful voice, someone like **Robyn** or **Lykke Li**. Indie-wise, I'd love to do something with **Muse**, **Friendly Fires**, Chris Martin from **Coldplay**, **Gary Barlow** would be good. Oh, and **Paul McCartney**!

The Song That Reminds Me Of My Big Year

I think you know what song this is going to be! Objectively though, it has to be **'Pass Out'**.

Knitwear - Christopher Kane
Shorts - Louis Vuitton
Glasses - Linda Farrow Luxe
Trainers - Nike Blazers

Downtime

There can be a lot of hanging round in the studio. Don't get me wrong, it's one of my favourite places to be, but when you're there for 20 hours, and it's like 5 a.m., and you're waiting for the engineer or producer to fiddle about with the drum parts for two hours, it can get a bit boring. So I like to keep myself amused with what's happening in the outside world: music, TV, comedians. I'm not so much into video games, but culturally, I like to try and keep up on what's what.

My Favourite Blogs

hypebeast.com
rwdmag.com – this is where I had one of my first features, and also my very first cover.
highsnobiety.com
datpiff.com
popjustice.com
punchbowlblog.com
soulculture.co.uk

My Favourite Comedians

Jimmy Carr
Ricky Gervais
Frankie Boyle
Russell Brand
Michael McIntyre – he's my absolute favourite.

My Favourite TV Shows

Prison Break
Family Guy
Luther
The Wire
Entourage
The Inbetweeners

Sometimes, I actually get to go home! When I am there, I'll be really honest – I like to tidy up! I find it really therapeutic. I don't get much time to myself at all, so I don't even have Sky, I just have Freeview. I don't really watch TV though and the only time I watch films or DVDs is on the tour bus really.

When I'm home, it's usually for a few hours' sleep and then I'm off again. I can cook though. I'll make some Nigerian food, some Jollof rice, chicken and beans.

If I had the time to work out, I would, but because of my schedule I don't. But hey, I jump around like a lunatic on stage, so doesn't that compensate for not pumping iron? Yeah, I think so!

Dating

One thing I'd love to have time for is going on dates with girls. But until life calms down, that just isn't going to happen. *BBM sad face*. I've had my fair share of experience though, and I think I've learnt a few lessons about dating girls...

Boys, when it comes to girls, here's my advice: be yourself, above everything. The chances are that if she does like you, you're going to have to maintain everything you put across when you first meet. The minute you change, that's when problems start. Tell her whatever's on your mind. However you feel about her, say it. If a girl's holding your hand and you don't like it, be honest. If you do like it, be honest. Just be yourself. Because if you don't say anything initially and then try broach the matter further down the line, then they are not going to be impressed!

When it comes to girls, I look for a number of things. I like a girl who's confident and has a great sense of humour. She has to have great fashion sense. I like a girl who takes pride in her appearance, has her hair and nails done nice. But appearance isn't as important as what's underneath. I've been on dates with some really beautiful girls, but if she takes herself too seriously, you're not going to get on.

The worst date I've ever had was with this one girl who literally interrogated me. I'd fancied her for ages, but she seemed to be too aware of what I do. She tried to come across as all, 'I'm not one of those girls, you know!' So she ended up interrogating me in an attempt to prove she wasn't impressed by me being a rapper. She was asking me if I styled my own clothes, if I'd changed the way I talk when I got famous, it was proper intrusive and rude. After a while I was just like, 'Why do I have to put up with this?' It was like a 60-minute *Newsnight* interview!

Like any boy, I've got a few celebrity crushes! I love Jameela Jamil, Rihanna, Freida Pinto, Zoe Saldana, Eva Mendes, and, I know everyone says her, but I love Kim Kardashian! I love Thandie Newton too – she's like a yummy mummy!

Glasses- Cutler and Gross
Shirt - Folk

Chapter
Seven:

GOING GLOBAL

*"Look where
we are. We've
done what we
thought we
couldn't."*

Disturbing The World

Without a doubt, one of the best things about working in music is that it allows you to travel all over the world. Like I was saying earlier, those high rises can block your horizons; when I moved into the semi-detached house in Plumstead it was like a whole new world of opportunity opened up to me. There was more to life than the estate. I think, in the back of my mind, I decided then and there that I wanted to see the world. I've been to a lot of different countries now, too many to list really. But there are still a few places I've not been to, though by the time you guys read this I will have been to Japan, and I hope to go to China and Brazil – but thanks to music I've travelled, literally, to the other side of the world and back.

Travelling has taught me, quite simply, that the world is a big place. There's so much to see, eat, hear and smell. Across the world I've seen some of the most beautiful beaches and spectacular architecture. I've met some incredible people and stayed in some fantastic hotels. On thing I do like to do though, wherever I go, is visit a city's ghetto. Whatever city you're in there's always a dilapidated, run-down area, or a shanty town. In LA, I saw an entire homeless family: a mum and dad, a daughter and a son all sat next to each other. It's crazy. The same day, I saw Quentin Tarantino hanging out in a private members' club. I think it's important to see all sides of life, and it's important to me to remind myself that not everybody can live a 'very wild lifestyle'. Far from it. Seeing how other people live is what really teaches me that about the world. The world is so big too, you need to get out there and see as much of it as you can. It can definitely influence you and make you a better person. It always amazes me too when I see people in other countries enjoying my music. It was always my aim to make music that people from any background can enjoy and on my travels I'm seeing that happen. It's unreal. Here are some of my travel highlights. Disturbing The World Baby!

Seeing how other people live is what really teaches me that about the world. The world is so big too, you need to get out there and see as much of it as you can.

WE DID EVERY SINGLE STATE YOU COULD NAME. WE PLAYED IN EVERY SMALL TOWN, EVERY MAJOR CITY.

Disturbing Ibiza

Ibiza is just always fun – flying around on speedboats in the sun, doing shows at infamous clubs like Space with people like Grandmaster Flash and Zane Lowe, or Pacha with Swedish House Mafia. It's just the best party place. It's always wild when we Disturb Ibiza!

Chipmunk and Skepta usually pop up. Once, I decided to play a little joke on Twitter with Skepta. He was in Majorca and he got so drunk that he gave Isaac and Charlesy his 'Boy Better Know' goldchain. 'I'm going to lose these chains, take them to Ibiza for me,' he said. I thought it would be funny to put up a ransom note on Twitter: 'If you want your chains back, meet me in Ibiza at 6 p.m. when the sun goes down.' It got so much attention. Later on that day, Skepta landed in Ibiza, 'I'm looking for a black guy, five foot nine, wearing two chains, if you see him, let me know!' We were both enjoying our success and poking fun at people who can be ignorant and think it's cool to rob people. I think it's nice for our fans to see us really enjoying the fruits of our labour.

Another time when I was doing Ibiza Rocks, Kylie came down to support me. We ended up staying up all night partying, until the sun came up! I had loads of energy to burn off though, the crowd had been so incredible that night, I was all hyped up and there was no way I could sleep that night. Kylie is the best person to go out partying with. She's so much fun.

> "I'll wake up in the morning with a mild case of amnesia."

Kylie is the best person to go out partying with. She's so much fun.

Disturbing France

The first time I got to go on a private jet was when I was doing a gig for Paris Hilton in the south of France. It was in March 2010 and I was supporting Rihanna in Glasgow. I got into a car and drove to a private airport and got a jet to Nice. From Nice, I got in a car to Cannes where I ran into a club, got changed in the dressing room and jumped straight on stage. I barely even said hello to Paris because straight after the performance, we flew from Nice back to Paris and then on to London City Airport. I just crashed out! This is what we call 'The worst best days of our lives'. It was amazing but awful because it's exhausting – between about 10 p.m. and 5 a.m. you take three flights, perform and drive for two hours. It's pretty tiring.

I've been on four private planes now and what happens is you wait in a little room with loads of fruit. It's all really nice and then the pilots come and introduce themselves, take your bags and they take you through security. They put your bag on the plane and then you get on. For some reason, there's always Marks & Spencer's sandwiches. I dunno why, but you always get them on private jets, in a little hamper thing! It's weird. Because the planes are so small though, when you hit a bit of turbulence you can really feel it. Luckily, I'm a good flyer!

I don't want to own a private jet myself, that's a bit out of my budget, but I look forward to the day when I can hire them myself. It's all leather seats, loads of room, nice and quiet, no waiting around in the airport. Let me tell you guys, it is the life!

For some reason, there's always Marks & Spencer's sandwiches. I dunno why, but you always get them on private jets, in a little hamper thing! It's weird.

Disturbing Australia

I went to Australia for Summadayze Festival in Perth, which was my first show of 2011. It was so incredible; N.E.R.D, David Guetta and Armand Van Helden were all playing too and that's when I ended up hanging out with Pharrell a lot. We had flown to New Zealand first, which took about 30 hours and then we had to jump on another flight to get to Australia. It was like the Blair Witch Project! I didn't know what was going on by the time we landed! I love the opportunity to travel to all these countries, it's incredible. And it helps when you fly Business Class! You eat some crazy food on your travels too. In Australia we had pancakes with bacon and banana! It sounds weird but it was good.

When you're on the go so much I like to just take five minutes to chill and put on a nice album – Adele's *21* is pretty perfect when you want to zone out. Before the festival, we went out on a boat on Sydney Harbour with Chromeo, Boys Noize and N.E.R.D where we had a little bonding session. That night we went to do the show, which was incredible. Me, Dumi, Isaac, the band, and Charlesy saw the New Year in watching N.E.R.D do the most incredible performance while drinking champagne. That's a New Year's Eve I'll never forget.

The best place I've been to so far, in fact, has been Australia. I went on tour with The Script out there and we became very good friends. Australia is great because it's so far away from home, but you still hear familiar voices everywhere you go. The people are really chilled out and they have a great way of life. They work hard but they also play hard. There's a beach every place you go. It's just gorgeous. It still has all the things that make London or New York great: nightlife, women, and good shops – but the weather's always great and the people are happier.

Australia is great because it's so far away from home, but you still hear familiar voices everywhere you go. The people are really chilled out and they have a great way of life.

Disturbing New Zealand

In New Zealand, I did this festival called Rhythm and Vines and it's one of the most memorable shows I've ever done. I was on the other side of the world – literally the furthest I could get away from Britain. There's nowhere else you can go after that. It's basically the end of the world! I was greeted by Maori warriors in their traditional way, where they close their eyes and they press their nose against yours. It was mad! But again, I was so grateful to be introduced to a whole new culture. Before the show, we went wine tasting and took a helicopter to take in all the beautiful scenery. It was magical. When it came to the show, I didn't know what to expect, I had no idea if the audience would know my songs, so we just decided to go out and have a good time. We got on stage and the sun was setting, and there was about 20,000 people on this big hill singing, jumping, going mad... It was one of the best sets of my life.

Disturbing The USA

America is a whole different ballgame. I wanted to make sure I wasn't trying to be something I'm not. That's always been my whole thing, but I didn't want to give America what they already have. I didn't want to go over and be all like, 'I'm the UK equivalent of Jay-Z or Kanye West.' Why do you want the equivalent when you've got the real deal already? Ultimately I was just trying to be Tinie Tempah.

It's hard to predict what song will work where, but 'Written In The Stars' was the one that the US loved. I think I had a song that people could relate to and it has a really good, positive message. You could hear it on radio stations everywhere around the world. It's good because I wanted to make that record, I wanted something that wasn't too poppy or too edgy, but that had universal appeal.

At the same time, what was going on back in the UK definitely helped. I made that transition from being an underground artist to winning Brits and Ivor Novellos and that helped carry my name across the Atlantic. Plus we did every single state you could name. We played in every small town, every major city. We were doing stuff for free for people, shaking hands, doing interviews with the same questions over and over... I took people out for dinner when I was there. I did everything, man!

The US is so difficult. I've been asked to do a full performance for just two people, almost like an audition. When you're a new act out there, you have to do more than just put the work in; you have to go over and above to deliver on every level. But I was absolutely determined. Wrestlemania played a big part too. They chose 'Written In The Stars' to be the official theme song for Wrestlemania 27, so it got an awful lot of media exposure and airplay. Millions of people watch Wrestlemania so that definitely helped.

When it got to No. 12, I was beside myself. No British rapper since Slick Rick had ever been taken seriously in America. Not only did I get to No. 12 in the Billboard Charts, but I was the first-ever British rapper to sell over a million singles

there. Can you imagine how that feels? It's thanks to so many elements: iSHi, Eric, me, the song itself, Dumi's hard work, the label, Wrestlemania... the planets aligned on that one and everything fell into place. It really was written in the stars!

When I first went over to America to work, I wanted to live in LA. I think I was blinded by the razzmatazz! My first trip was pre-Grammy week and I saw Quentin Tarantino, Lil Wayne, Lionel Richie. I was like, 'Rah.' The weather was amazing, it was just ridiculous, crazy. But New York feels like it's got a lot more culture and is a more honest place. It's a lot closer to home in terms of flying. New York is a lot like Britain too; New Yorkers seems to have a lot more depth and character to them. And the fashion is pretty crazy. It suits me as a city. I could definitely do six months or a year in America.

Although, after spending time there, I finally understood why everyone drinks so much coffee – in a city that never sleeps, something has to keep you awake! The food is a major thing too. I always eat a lot of pancakes in America. But then I started experimenting and making my own. I'd get the pancakes and instead of syrup, I'll have bacon, eggs, spinach. The weirdest thing is that they don't have baked beans. They don't even know what they are! I get withdrawal symptoms from beans and tea after a while. I asked for tea once and they came back with two jugs of ice-cold tea! It even had a lemon in it. No thanks, mate!

What happened to me in Britain after I first got signed seems to be repeating itself in the US now. I've started being here, there and everywhere – TV, radio and everything.

I'm glad I had the chance to do Graham Norton before I got to America, because it helped to prepare me for doing the huge TV shows. Chat shows like Jay Leno get massive audiences – bigger than anything in Britain, but thankfully I'd had some practice by then. I was nervous, but excited. Everyone was saying bad things about Jay Leno before I met him, but he turned out to be the nicest guy. He gave me a chessboard and then he drew me a picture and signed it for me! It was weird but cool. He was wearing double denim – do you believe that? Imagine Jay Leno in

double denim! The other thing that amazed me was that he has a car for every day of the year. He has 365 cars and keeps them in an airplane hanger!

David Letterman was another big deal. But his studio is freezing! I've never been in a single room that was as cold as that one. If you watch my performance I'm wearing like a leather jacket, a hoodie and a shirt! He has it so cold so he doesn't sweat and apparently it helps to keep the audience awake and alert, too.

Another big step was doing my first US festival – Coachella! It's a really key festival for breaking not only American acts, but also music from around the world. Every major journalist, DJ, artist is there and also thousands and thousands of hardcore music fans. We just wanted to make a bit of history; it was so hot, and it was a lot of work but I just wanted to kill it cos once you kill Coachella, you've done it. It was mad, Clint Eastwood was there, I met David Hasselhoff, I caught up with Usher and saw Pharrell again too. It's the most incredible place, out in the desert, all these celebrities everywhere and some of the most amazing live music you will see in your life. I'd love to play Coachella every year if I could.

I feel like I'm making a lot of headway in America and I just hope it continues. After the success of 'Written in the Stars', we realised we had to strike while the iron was hot, as it were. But I didn't want to get a random collaboration with an American rapper I'd never met or had any connection with. I wanted something that felt natural. That's when me and Wiz Khalifa teamed up. The relationship between us built up quite naturally. He'd heard my remix of his single, 'Black and Yellow', and he liked it and asked if I could make it official. So we swapped tracks. He had laid down an idea for the chorus, I heard it and liked it and that's how it came about. I really related to the lyrics of 'Til I'm Gone' because it talks about how success can come very quickly; one moment you're in your house making mixtapes and then next you're travelling across the world performing songs. It felt so relevant. All the crazy experiences I've had, wanting to be the best I could be and make something crazy out in America, it spoke about all that! I just hope my American dream really does come true. But my heart will always be at home in south London!

once you kill Coachella, you've done it... It was mad, Clint Eastwood was there, I met David Hasselhoff, and caught up with Usher.

I finally understood why everyone drinks so much coffee - in a city that never sleeps, something has to keep you awake!

MEMORIAL DAY WEEKEND 5/27-5/29
PAUL VAN DYK,   PAUL OAKENFOLD,
FELIX DA HOUSECAT, TINIE TEMPAH,
YELAWOLF, CHROMEO,
MORGAN PAGE & GREEN VELVET
FOR TICKETS & INFO THELOVEFESTIVAL.COM

THE NEXT CHAPTER

DAMN, I CAN'T BELIEVE WE'VE NEARLY COME TO THE END!

One More Thing

Looking over these pages reminds me of how much has happened, particularly in the last two years. Now I'm here and I've been given the opportunity, I'm seriously not messing around. Yes, I live somewhere nice, but it's not nice enough. Yes, the album's done, but now I want to do another one. I want another No.1, I want a Grammy, I want to collaborate with Kanye and Jay-Z. Basically, I've got a lot to do.

I was hanging out with Benji from Good Charlotte in LA – as you do! – and he said to me, 'Do you know what I like about you man? You don't go into 'rapper mode'. You don't see people and start acting weird; if you want to laugh at something silly, you just do it.' And I think that's always been the case. There has never been a plan about who I 'should' be or what I 'should' rap about. If I'm doing an interview, I don't think in the back of my mind, I have to be 'cool', I just go for it and I think people connected with that. What you see is what you get.

My thing is that you can put up a façade to be whoever you want to be, but if it works out for you, you're going to have to maintain that for the rest of your career and that's a lot of work. So why not just be yourself? And that's what I've stuck to doing. It's worked okay so far!

The best thing about being Tinie Tempah is that I'm getting to live my dream. Literally to the 'T', exactly how I wanted it. I'm happy, my family is healthy, I'm surrounded by the best people you could ask for. I genuinely feel love and respect from my fans and the scene I came from. I have pride in Britain. It was the best when I won the Brit and I was told by everyone that they shared a sense of genuine love and excitement. Me and Dumi and the whole team, we've kept to ourselves and put our heads down to do what we set out to do. We don't feel we owe anyone anything but at the same time we've paid our dues, you know? We've been able to do things a lot of MCs haven't done yet and that's a satisfying feeling.

I think the secret to my success is that I've always been insanely optimistic. I definitely believe that if you wanna do something wholeheartedly, believe it and

work hard towards it, you can do it. That's the secret. I've always remembered my 'pleases' and 'thank yous' everywhere I've gone. I have always tried my best to make music that's realistic. I think I understood pop music, and I had a go at making it the way I saw fit to do so. People respond to that. My personality might have helped too. Trying to always be chirpy and up for anything, that's part of it as well.

Next up, I definitely want to be nominated for a Grammy. I'd love for album two to go triple platinum. I'm so excited for you guys to hear it. Pharrell has produced some tracks, I've been in the studio with Usher, I'm talking to Adele about doing something, I'm working with The Script. There's a few amazing British and American artists that no one would expect me to work with but out of coincidence we've met and I've taken their number and we've sent some ideas around. I can't wait to try that stuff out. It's gonna hopefully be something truly brilliant. Everything that's going on now is going to be reflected in my new album. What's happening at home, what fame can do to people, what money can do to people around you, I'll be talking about all of that. My music is made in real time – *Disc-Overy* was about discovering myself and the industry and my life in general. The next album will be, 'I'm here now, I'm battling to stay sane.' I don't know how to explain it. It gets overwhelming and being a creative person, you realise how much PR and politics are involved in being a musician. Half the job is just selling yourself; it's not all the music itself. Adele is the only person I know who does such minimal promo, she lets the music do the work. But for most artists – Lady Gaga, Beyoncé, Katy Perry, Jay-Z – it's about the brand you become and a lot of that thinking has gone into the new record.

The last two years have been a great ride though; there have been good times, embarrassing times, awkward times... I don't think I've changed as a person but all these things have been life lessons. I want to reflect the next stage of my life in my next record.

There have been so many highlights: No. 1s, Snoop, Dizzee telling me he was proud of me. Prince William coming to watch my set at the Radio 1 Weekender,

entering the charts in America... so many. I feel very, very fortunate and I couldn't have done this without the help of you guys.

The main, biggest, best highlight was actually going back to my old school, St Paul's, for the first time since getting my results. Lessons stopped and everyone came out, I went and said 'Hello' and it was pandemonium. Then they took me to a new part of the school and guess what was there? A brand-new studio opened in my name. Seeing that definitely topped the highlights.

I looked around at the kids and could suddenly see myself when I was their age with my whole future stretched out before me. I just hope that studio helps some of them to achieve the things they want to achieve too.

Thanks for buying this book and for taking the time out to read it. Who would have thought, eh? Clothing lines, singles, albums, collaborations and now my very own book! This has been an amazing experience, being able to relive all these amazing memories.

Finally, I want to tell you guys one more thing. I love my fans. I love you more than you can imagine. If it wasn't for you, I wouldn't have got to where I am, especially so quickly. You're my support structure. You've helped me through things you wouldn't imagine. When times were hard, you kept me on my feet. I just want to thank you so much.

Hopefully, this is the first chapter of a long and exciting story and I'll look forward to writing more exciting tales to come! I can't wait to see you all as we continue down the road together. Me and you, we've still a got a lot to do. Disturbing The Universe, Baby! We've only just begun.

I'd like to thank Mum, Dad, Kelly, Marian and Kelvin for all of the amazingly accurate information provided. Dumi, Richie, Isaac, Mitchell and Tev, All About She and everyone at Disturbing London for capturing some of the most amazing moments of my life on camera and in their memories, helping me to recall them. Hattie Collins for editing all the 'innits' and 'dy'u know what I means' into the most beautiful flowing story every written. St Francis Primary, St Patrick's Primary, St Paul's Secondary and St Francis Xavier Sixth Form for nurturing and educating me, and helping me become the person I am today. Grime music and all its pioneers for giving me a passion and something to believe in. Obi, Billy and everyone at WME for getting me the most amazing gigs all over the world, allowing me to work with artists I've always dreamed of. Tobi, Josh and everyone at Eight28 for making sure all of those shows went as planned. Lol. Miles and Nathan for helping me sign, seal and deliver. Janet and Emma G for helping people get to know the real me and always portraying me in the best light and most positive way. Everyone at Parlophone and Capitol for making sure this worked. All of those extra hours in the office are paying off guys. Ellie, Chip, Diddy, JLS, Example, Eliza, Wiz and Joe for saying such nice things about me in my book. I'm chuffed! Kelly and everyone at Ebury, and David and everyone at Method UK, for seeing the vision and being extremely patient down to the very last minute. Haha. And last, but most importantly, you for reading this book from the very start all the way to here. I hope you have learnt a little bit more about me and also learnt that anything is possible and I stand by that very firmly. Put your mind to it, work extra hard, keep good intentions and you will get everything you want out of life, I promise! Until next time, sayonara suckers! :-P

Credits

Designed by David Pitt at Method UK

PICTURE CREDITS

End Papers
Rowan Miles/EMPICS Entertainment/Press Association Images

Intro
Page 2 – 3 Tracey Nearmy/Press Association Images
Page 5 Adam Lawrence
Page 6 – 7 Adam Lawrence
Page 9 Adam Lawrence
Page 10 – 11 Adam Lawrence

Chapter One
Page 12 – 13 Frank Hoensch/Getty Images
Page 26 Ryan McVay/Getty Images

Chapter Two
Page 43 Eleanor Bentall/Corbis

Chapter Three
Page 42 – 43 Yui Mok/Press Association Images
Page 49 Yui Mok/Press Association Images
Page 51 Top Left: Yui Mok/Press Association Images
Top Right: Yui Mok/Press Association Images
Bottom Right: Duncan Bryceland/Rex Features

Page 52 Top Left: Action Press/Rex Features
Top Right: Rex Features
Bottom Left: Mark Allan/Press Association Images
Page 53 Top Right: Brian Rasic/Rex Features
Centre: Brian Rasic/Rex Features
Bottom Left: Press Association Images
Bottom Right: Brian Rasic/Rex Features
Page 55 Rowan Miles/EMPICS Entertainment/Press Association Images
Page 56 The Times/NI Syndication
Page 60 All: Adam Lawrence
Page 61 Centre Left: Dave M. Benett/Getty Images
Centre Right: Andre Csillag/Rex Features
Bottom Left: John Phillips/Press Association Images
Bottom Right: Yui Mok/Press Association
Page 64 Top: Dave M. Benett/Getty Images
Centre: Matt Kent/Getty Images
Bottom Centre: Ian West/Press Association Images
Bottom Right: Rex Features
Page 65 Top: Suzan/Press Association Images

All other photographs are the author's own

'Snap' Words and Music by Patrick Okogwu, Eshraque Mughal, M Asari, T Riley, Abdel-Karim Lasfirare (c) 2010, Reproduced by Permission of EMI Music Publishing Ltd, London W8 5SW

'Written In The Stars' Words and Music by Patrick Okogwu, Words and Music by Patrick Okogwu, Charlie Bernando, Eric Turner (c) 2010, Reproduced by Permission of EMI Music Publishing Ltd, London W8 5SW

'Frisky' Words and Music by Patrick Okogwu, Timothy McKenzie, Marc Williams (c) 2010, Reproduced by Permission of EMI Music Publishing Ltd, London W8 5SW

'Miami 2 Ibiza' Words and Music by Patrick Okogwu, Steve Angello, Axel Hedfors, Sebastian Ingrosso (c) 2010, Reproduced by Permission of EMI Music Publishing Ltd, London W8 5SW

'Obsession' Words and Music by Patrick Okogwu, Emile Hayne (c) 2010, Reproduced by Permission of EMI Music Publishing Ltd, London W8 5SW

'Invincible' Words and Music by Patrick Okogwu, Eshraque Mughal, Philipe Marc Anquetil (c) 2010, Reproduced by Permission of EMI Music Publishing Ltd, London W8 5SW

'Wonderman' Words and Music by Patrick Okogwu, Timothy McKenzie, Marc Williams (c) 2010, Reproduced by Permission of EMI Music Publishing Ltd, London W8 5SW

'Let Go' Words and Music by Patrick Okogwu, Ben Harrison, S Khan, Emile Hayne (c) 2010, Reproduced by Permission of EMI Music Publishing Ltd, London W8 5SW